Pioneering with
Wildflowers

DEDICATED

to Peter Rabbit in the hope that flattery will accomplish what traps and guns have failed to do and that the little rascal will let our plants alone from this time on.

Pioneering with
Wildflowers

by George D. Aiken

Foreword by Henry W. Art

Illustrated by Marion Satterlee

Alan C. Hood & Company, Inc.
BRATTLEBORO, VERMONT

Pioneering with Wildflowers

Copyright © 1935, 1963, 1968, 1978 by George D. Aiken

Published by arrangement with The Countryman Press. Inc.

Manufactured in United States of America.

Published by Alan C. Hood & Co., Inc.
Brattleboro, Vermont 05301.

Library of Congress Cataloging-in-Publication Data

Aiken, George D. (George David), 1892-1984.

Pioneering with wildflowers / by George D. Aiken ; foreword by Henry
W. Art ; illustrated by Marion Satterlee.
    p.   cm.
Originally published: Rochester, N.Y. : Genesee Press, c 1933.
Includes indexes.

    1. Wildflower gardening.   2. Wild flowers — United States.
I. Title.
SB439.A5   1994
635.9'517 — dc20   94-4530
                                                          CIP

ISBN 0-911469-11-7

10 9 8 7 6 5 4 3 2 1

An Important Message from the Publisher

Certain species of wildflowers are protected under the law and should not be taken from the wild. These include ladyslippers and trilliums, especially the Pink Ladyslipper (*Cypripedium acaule*) and the Snow or White Trillium (*Trillium grandiflorum*). Although some nurseries sell plants of these species and call them "nursery-grown," they are often actually gathered from the wild and kept in nursery holding areas for no more than several weeks or months. Commercial propagation of these species is not feasible, and gardeners should avoid buying such specimens. Please see paragraphs 4 and 5 of the Foreword by Henry W. Art.

Foreword

By Henry W. Art

It is with enthusiasm akin to that of seeing the reemergence of spring flowers that the republication of George Aiken's classic book is greeted. *Pioneering with Wildflowers* is itself a pioneering work of great importance that deserves to be read by a new generation of native plant lovers. Like Senator Aiken himself, this book is a sturdy, reliable, insightful and highly personal work that connects gardeners to their local environments and beyond.

If George Aiken were alive today, he would be 101 years old and undoubtedly his unabashed love for native plants would be undiminished from that of sixty years ago when he wrote *Pioneering with Wildflowers*. This is one of the first books that concentrated on native plants as fitting materials for gardens. The book drew upon the practical experience of Aiken's ground-breaking work with wildflowers at his Putney Nursery in Putney, Vermont.

Those times were both different from and the same as today. Aiken is clear in his motivations for writing this book — that people should know how to propagate and grow native plants rather that resorting to digging them in the wild. He was alarmed at the reduction in native plant populations that resulted from the depredations of wild collecting in his day. The need for public education about growing wildflowers is even greater today than it was in the 1930s.

Although the book remains remarkably current and vital in its attention to environmental conditions such as drainage, pH, temperature and the light that native species require for their growth, today's reader should be aware that great caution is needed in the incorporation of certain species in the garden. In particular, the propagation of lady-slipper orchids by commercial growers has proven to be elusive. George Aiken may have been successful in this endeavor, but if so, his feat is like the lost art of medieval stained glass production, which escapes modern technology. According to the New England Wildflower Society and the Eastern Native Plant Alliance, virtually all the lady-slippers, such as *Cypripedium acaule*, in the plant trade are wild-collected rather then nursery-

---

HENRY W. ART is Samuel Fessenden Clarke Professor of Biology, Williams College and author of A GARDEN OF WILDFLOWERS (Garden Way Publishing) and THE WILDFLOWER GARDENER'S GUIDES (Garden Way Publishing).

propagated. It is therefore best to avoid purchasing these plants at all, and should you be fortunate enough to find some growing on your property, do not move them, but rather plan your garden around them!

Care should be used when purchasing any native plants from garden centers or by mail, especially lilies, trilliums, trout lilies, and other bulbs. These natives take a long time to reach flowering size and therefore should be relatively expensive. Make sure that the plants have been "nursery-propagated," that is, grown from seeds or divisions by a professional propagator. Some suppliers list natives as "nursery-grown," which sometimes means that plants have been dug in the wild and merely grown in a pot or nursery bed for a period of time. A directory of reputable wild-flower nurseries is published by the New England Wildflower Society (180 Hemenway Road, Framingham, MA 01701-2699).

Only a couple of the species mentioned by Aiken should be avoided entirely. Purple loosestrife (*Lythrum salicaria*) has now proved to be a noxious and overly aggressive, invasive weed that is displacing significant populations of native wetland species. There are no truly sterile hybrids of this alien species, so do not plant it. Bitter nightshade (*Solanum dulcamara*) might well also be avoided, since it has poisonous berries and a tendency towards rank growth.

The reader will find that the scientific names of a few plants have changed over the past half-century. While taxonomists have been busy changing some of the Latin names [see Index, pages 135-145], however, the common names have remained essentially the same.

The need to live in harmony with one's surroundings is a clear message of this friendly work. As you become familiar with the species that Aiken describes and enlivens with deserved personalities, you will gain renewed appreciation for them. *Pioneering with Wildflowers* is a handy book for taking out into the garden with you or to curl up with on a cold winter's night as you contemplate the renewal of the spring beauties in the coming May.

HENRY W. ART
Williamstown, Mass.
September, 1993

Introduction

THREE hundred years ago the North American continent was an unknown wilderness, peopled by a primitive race and replete with an abundance of wild animal and plant life. Then, as the hardy and adventurous pioneers of the old world sought out our shores in great numbers, the native Americans, people, animals, and plants, were crowded back, slowly at first, but with ever increasing rapidity until now only a small fraction of their former number remains.

What a paradise of wildflowers the early pioneers must have found. And, looking at some of these flowers, I can see the pages of history turn backward and visualize those who gazed upon them for the first time.

In the Showy Ladyslipper, I see the Jesuits of France, their canoes breasting the currents of mighty rivers, as they plunge deeper and deeper into the forests to establish the outposts of civilization in the far flung recesses of the vast Canadian wilderness.

The Poppy Mallow, sprawling with brilliant splashes of color on the sun baked Western plains, presents long lines of covered wagons, creeping scarcely faster than the Mallow itself, as homeseekers risk all to follow the sunset to their promised land.

And the Hepaticas, Bloodroots, Violets and Columbine, in them is colonial New England—school days, homemade clothes and bare feet, the bunch of flowers shyly placed on the teacher's desk, childhood games, laughter and sorrow.

Yes, the wildflowers have seen the development of the comforts of our so-called civilization. They have seen the forests cut away, cities and villages grow up, roads made, bogs and marshes drained for agricultural purposes, great reservoirs built, flooding the fertile basins, and with each new development they have suffered.

Constantly pushed back by immigrant people, immigrant animals, and even immigrant plants, many species are now making a gallant last stand in the face of extermination. If some of them are to be saved, it must be through the prompt action of our people. We must learn how to propagate and grow all worthwhile species, and the purpose of this book is to give others, in plain, non-technical language some of the knowledge of wildflower requirements which I have learned during the last ten years.

The old frontier days of America are over, but the last stand of some of our wildflowers presents to us a new frontier in which we can adventure and that is why I call this book, "Pioneering with Wildflowers."

GEORGE D. AIKEN

Contents

Chapter		Page
I.	Why Grow Wildflowers?	1
II.	Who Should Grow Wildflowers?	4
III.	Soils and Environment	6
IV.	Propagation and Planting	10
V.	The Ladyslippers	17
VI.	The Fringe-Orchids	23
VII.	Little Bog Orchids	27
VIII.	Other Orchids	29
IX.	Trailing Arbutus	31
X.	Violets	35
XI.	Two Months of Trilliums	39
XII.	Along the Woodland Pathway	43
XIII.	The Woodland Rock Garden	51
XIV.	Color on the Hillside	57
XV.	Some Plants With Bright Berries	65
XVI.	Our Native Phlox	70
XVII.	Wild Lilies	73
XVIII.	Flowers of the Fields	75
XIX.	Roadside Neighbors	83
XX.	The Glory of the Bogs	89
XXI.	Ponds and Streams	95
XXII.	Plants for the Marshes	101
XXIII.	Nature Lays a Carpet	105
XXIV.	Ogres of the Bogs	111
XXV.	Fringed Gentian	115
XXVI.	Wild Asters	119
XXVII.	A Little Desert	121
XXVIII.	Ferns	125

CHAPTER I

Why Grow Wildflowers?

⇶ ⇶ ⇷ ⇷

IN the farthest corner of my father's pasture was a small wood lot of sugar maples, birches, hop hornbeam and pignut hickory, growing on rocky, ledgy ground. The cows were usually turned out to pasture the last of April and it was my work and that of old Shep to get them down to the bars in time for milking every night. Usually their bovine obstinacy would prompt them to linger in this small wood lot in the far end of the pasture to make Shep and me as much work as possible in getting them. But in this little grove of hardwoods there were quantities of Springbeauties, Hepaticas, Bloodroot, Violets, Squirrelcorn and Dutchmans-breeches, which so entranced the young man of eight years that it was occasionally necessary for some older member of the family to not only come after the cows, but Shep and me as well.

One night I dug and brought home a clump of Dutchmans-breeches and planted it under the lilac bush. I know now that blossoming time is not the proper time to move Dutchmans-breeches, but Providence looks after those who know no better, and that clump lived in its new home for nearly twenty years before the suckers of the lilac finally obliterated it. This was the first wild gardening I ever did.

It has been a good many years since I have been after the cows and listened to the silent but impressive sermons preached by Jack-in-the-pulpit or stained my face and hands with the juice of the wild wood strawberries, but the friendly feeling for the wild things of the woods and fields which I acquired in those philosophical younger days has persisted. I always regarded the wildflowers of the woods as members of the family and rather felt it my duty to look after them as far as possible, while they in turn would impart many secrets which could never be learned inside the schoolhouse walls.

1

Great changes have taken place in our New England hills since I moved that clump of Dutchmans-breeches. Groves of great trees, under whose branches the dainty people of the woods lived and thrived, have been cut for lumber, and in their place is a maze of young growth so thick that only here and there are the wildflowers, formerly so abundant, able to survive. The open pastures are being covered with sapling growth of birches and pine not yet old enough to furnish shade and shelter for our woodland flowers, but just large enough to choke out the flowers of the open fields.

Even the people are changing. Formerly the hillside farms in New England were occupied by hardworking Yankee farmers, who struggled so industriously to wrest a living from the land that they had scant time to enjoy the beauties of the wildflowers. These farms are now being rapidly occupied by folks from the cities, good folks—most of them, but still folks who take such pride in the ownership of land in the country that they are prone to nail up "No trespassing" signs on every corner.

And then our roads. They are better, much better than we used to have, but this very fact has had disastrous results for many of our wildflower neighbors. Even from distant cities the automobile brings friends and relatives to the farmer's home on Sunday afternoon and when they leave the back of the car may be laden with, besides tired human beings, masses of Laurel, Azaleas, Columbine or Arbutus, and our roadsides become so much poorer. I would not for an instant deny the people the right to enjoy and love our wildflowers, but the sad part of the story is that the loveliest wildflowers are being almost exterminated in the most accessible places.

What are we going to do about it? Well, some of us have spent a great many years thinking over this problem. Passing laws does not do any good because with the permission of the landowner anyone may gather wildflowers under the protection of the Constitution. Posting land on the part of estate owners may preserve these plants, but where they may be enjoyed by comparatively few people.

I believe that all human people need close association with Nature's people, so it seems to me that the only satisfactory answer to this problem is to tell folks how to grow them.

In this book I am undoubtedly making statements about which I shall have to revise my opinion within a few years, but it is the very fact that we have so little information available on this subject that makes it so intensely interesting. Mistakes are inevitable. Failures may be more prevalent than successes, but if in failing one finds the reason for the failure the work has been worthwhile.

CHAPTER II

Who Should Grow Wildflowers?

-»» -»» «« ««-

THE question is often asked me as to who should attempt growing wildflowers. My answer is anyone who likes them well enough to take care of them, for there are species of North American plants that will thrive under almost any conditions if given reasonable attention.

The estate owners may use these plants by the tens of thousands for naturalizing along the woodland pathway, the open fields, or the borders of streams and ponds.

Then we have the city dweller who may have no land at all, or at the most a tiny backyard. More and more miniature wild gardens have come into being in the cities, not only in the backyards and on the roofs, but even tiny indoor gardens or window box gardens, where the urban dweller, by watching them unfold their leaves and develop their blossoms, can in imagination take delightful trips through fields and woods, up mountains and across meadows.

Within recent years there have been established many wildflower preserves where the aim is to grow as many species as possible so students and others who are unable to take long trips through the country may see them and study them. This work should be encouraged, for it not only provides a means by which our people may become acquainted with our wildflowers, but also, if properly taken care of, insures the perpetuation and a source of seed supply of many rare and unusual varieties.

What a wonderful thing it would be if just outside every city or large town there could be established a wildflower preserve. People could be taught not only how to grow the plants, but also how to gather the flowers without injury to the future supply. They could learn how useless it is to try to transplant certain species into the wrong location or at the wrong time of the year. They could learn how to cut the blossoms of Azaleas and Mountain Laurel so that instead of ruining the

4

bushes they would become thriftier and more free blooming than ever, how Princess Pine may be gathered without doing the least harm, and so many other things they ought to know.

After all, Nature has given us the wild things to enjoy and when we see children, or even grown-ups, thoughtlessly gathering flowers and plants because they have the natural human love for them, but which will result in disaster for the plants, isn't it better to explain to them the futility of what they are attempting and the resultant loss to everyone than to berate them for their ignorance?

Wildflowers are used in the gardens of the village or farm, either appropriately intermingled with other flowers or occupying a wild corner by themselves, perhaps under an apple tree whose shade will make the forest flowers feel at home. It is in these home gardens that much of the experimental work in propagating and growing native plants has been done, for while the estate owner is likely to leave the care of the plants to hired employees and the city dweller with his tiny wild garden may lack facilities for carrying on the work, the suburban or farm gardener is more intimately acquainted with the characteristics of each species. He cares for them himself, notices their faults and virtues and has greater opportunity for giving each species its desired environment.

CHAPTER III

Soils and Environment

-->>- -->>- -<<- -<<-

IN making natural plantings or in establishing wildflower gardens one should make conditions for each species as nearly as possible like those of the place where the plant grows naturally. In regard to soil, drainage and amount of shade no fixed rules can be made, however, because of the extremely variable local conditions and also from the fact that certain plants grow under different conditions in different parts of the country. Many species which in the South almost invariably grow in shade will do nicely in full sun in the North, and by the same reasoning some of our New England plants which grow in full sun prefer a little shade when they are taken to sections where the summers are longer and hotter.

Another reason why fixed rules cannot be laid down is because the growing of wildflowers is so very much in the pioneer stage at present that after growing certain plants for several years successfully, attributing our success to certain conditions, we sometimes discover, against our will, that there may be an altogether different reason for it.

Only a few years ago it was thought that the secret of growing native plants successfully depended largely upon the amount of acid in the soil. It is undoubtedly true that many do require much more acid than others, but only within the last two years I have come to believe that acidity of the soil, while being a powerful influence, may not be the primary reason for success or failure. As an example, take the Walking Leaf Fern, Wild Blue Phlox, Meadow Lily, Twinleaf and American Columbine, all of which have been thought to require either neutral or slightly alkaline soil. I find from experience that these plants will grow luxuriantly in intensely acid soil if they are given dense shade. Not being scientist enough to explain the reason for this I will leave the answer to my readers.

On the other hand some plants apparently resent the intensely acid soil regardless of shade conditions. A conspicuous example of this is the Sharplobe Hepatica (Hepatica acutiloba), which has refused to thrive in very acid soil regardless of the amount of shade.

The principal species of native plants which seemingly demand very acid conditions are the Clintonia, Trailing Arbutus, Wood Lily, Bunchberry, Moccasin Flower, Pitcherplants, Goldthread, Checkerberry, Galax, Oconee Bells, Roundlobe Hepatica, Iris verna, Twinflower, Creeping Snowberry, Foamflower, Painted Trillium and Creeping Phlox.

Plants besides the Sharplobe Hepatica apparently insisting on soil that is neutral or containing very little acid are the Fringed Gentian, Showy Orchis, Shootingstar and Early Saxifrage.

Much as I dislike to criticise the assertions of some of our chemists and horticulturists in regard to certain degrees of acidity of the soil being necessary for the successful growing of various plant species, yet I must frankly say that I think this has been over emphasized, and while the degree of acidity undoubtedly determines the success of our ericaceous shrubs and some wildflowers, yet it seems to be a secondary and not primary factor in successfully growing most of our native plants.

One of the most necessary things to consider is the matter of drainage. There are very few wild plants that will thrive in soil that is not well drained. Even most of our bog plants require good drainage. A sure way to fail with such plants as the Showy and Yellow Ladyslippers is to plant them in muck or any place where the water stands around the crowns during part of the year. Nature invariably plants them upon the hummocks where the crowns are always high and dry, but the roots may grow down through these hummocks until they reach perpetually moist ground from which to draw a generous supply of water.

Shade is a matter for prime consideration, for upon the quality of the shade may depend the success or failure of a plant species.

The shade of an old sugar maple tree is not a desirable location for a wildflower garden because the roots of the maple will rob the plants of the moisture which they should have. No matter how much one works to cut out the fibrous roots of the maple and to prepare a spot with fresh soil from the woods, it is only a question of time before the tree will send new roots thicker than ever right into the specially prepared soil and rob the wildflowers. True, they grow freely in the hardwoods where sugar maples are abundant, but the maple in the backyard is a different proposition.

If no other spot is available, however, I would advise putting not less than eighteen inches of new soil on the top of the ground where the wild garden is to be. By doing this and by watering liberally when needed, one may be successful.

Under an old apple tree a wild garden can usually be successfully made. This is also true of such trees as the elm and locust. If only conifers—pine and hemlock—are available for shade the number of species of wildflowers that can be grown will necessarily be limited to those which tolerate acid soil, as the falling needles will soon make the soil very sour.

The shade of a building often provides a satisfactory site for a wild garden, but here one confronts the problem of water dripping from the eaves and snow and ice sliding from the roof in winter. If there is no danger from this source, the north side of a building may be transformed into a miniature forest fairyland.

But the best shade of all is artificial shade. When I first started growing wildflowers commercially, we used to make beds in the woods where the flowers were found growing naturally and propagate them right there. But, regardless of the kinds of trees there were, they would, in a couple of years' time, take possession of these beds and fill them completely with their fibrous roots. So it became necessary, as our plantings got more extensive, to provide a different and more concentrated location.

We built our artificial shade house by using locust posts cut eleven feet long. These were put in the ground three feet deep and ten feet apart each way. Cross pieces were run from post to post and brush from the wood lot woven across the top, the amount depending upon how dense we needed the shade for that particular spot. Birches cut in early summer provided the most and best shade for least expense because the leaves drying on them gave a most natural effect and, being slender, they wove easily into the framework of the shade house.

At one time we tried evergreen boughs, but one experience was enough. The needles were continually dropping down one's neck as he walked underneath and also tended to greatly increase the acidity of the soil. If the city dweller finds it impossible to secure brush for a shade house he can obtain practically the same effect by the use of common lath.

By building a house of this nature we were able to provide the necessary amount of shade for each species of wildflower and to furnish it without having to combat the roots of the trees, which were so ravenous in the forest beds.

Having furnished the roof of the shade house we next constructed the beds. These were all raised to provide drainage and enclosed in board sides for better control of the soil mixtures. In the bottom of these beds we filled in three or four inches of cobble stones and pieces of stumps, rotten wood, and roots screened from the leafmold, to provide perfect drainage. On the top of this we placed several inches of soil mixture, sweet or sour, sandy, clayey or loamy, according to the desires of the species of plant to be set in each bed. By this method plants with very different requirements can be grown side by side, which is economically advantageous.

Providing water for wildflowers is of great importance. An underground pipe leading directly to the wild garden with a stand pipe to which a hose may be attached is perhaps the easiest method. In growing marsh or bog plants an underground pipe may be arranged from which the water can flow a few inches below the surface of the ground.

The soil for the various wildflowers should be made as nearly as possible like the natural soil in which the plant grows. Practically all plants of the forest require leafmold in some form. The acid-loving plants will thrive if commercial granulated peat moss is mixed with the soil, but the plants from the hardwoods forest greatly prefer the natural leafmold from beeches and maples. For the first few years after beech and maple leaves fall they seem to be alkaline, but as one gets below these layers of leaves into the older mold it tends to be acid.

I strongly disapprove of burning leaves. They are Nature's fertilizer and should be made into compost heaps. When mixed with garden soil and, if possible, some well rotted cow manure they form a fertilizer which appeals to almost any plant that grows.

CHAPTER IV

Propagation and Planting

THERE are several different methods by which the supply of wild-flowers, like the cultivated plants of the garden, may be increased, but the principal methods are by growing from seed, by softwood or root cuttings, by layering and by division.

PROPAGATION BY SEED. Nature propagates all wildflowers by seed except some abortive kinds such as Double Bloodroot or the Double Trillium, which refuse to make seed at all. For nearly all kinds man adopts the commonest method of Nature, but sometimes tries to do the work without observing closely enough the conditions under which Nature performs.

In growing wild plants from seed one should follow the same general rules as in growing any hardy perennials. The soil should be thoroughly sifted and cleaned of sticks, roots and stones. For most species a generous addition of sand to the seeding soil seems to aid germination and often a mixture of equal parts of sand, screened leafmold, either acid or neutral, according to the requirements of the plant, and soil will be found to be satisfactory. The depth to which seed should be planted will depend upon the size of the seed and one must use ordinary judgment in this matter.

Having sown the seed, preferably in flats for fine growing varieties, but in open beds for coarser species like Jack-in-the-pulpit and Bane-berries, it is necessary to protect them from washing and the drip from the brush roof. A piece of burlap laid directly upon the soil will accomplish this effect with the coarser seeds, but be sure to watch constantly when they are germinating. Otherwise the young plants will grow up through the burlap and it will be impossible to remove either the burlap or the plants without disastrous results.

The finer seeds, such as those of Gentians, are best covered with glass

10

to completely exclude the rain. After the seed is sown the soil should be kept moist according to the desire of the species there sown.

The time of sowing varies greatly with the species. Trailing Arbutus and Fringed Gentian give best results if sown as soon as ripe. If the seed of the Greek-valerian, however, is sown as soon as ripe in midsummer it has been my experience that it will not come up until the following spring and therefore it is better to wait until late fall or spring before sowing it.

Seeds with hard shells, such as Baneberries and Trilliums, should be sown in autumn to permit them to stratify during the winter. And even then they may require two years for germination. The seed of the Plumy Bleedingheart germinates so readily and grows so rapidly that if sown when ripe in midsummer it will produce salable plants the following spring.

If one has no facilities for growing plants at home, very successful results may be obtained with the larger seeded species by gathering them when ripe and sowing in the soil around the mother plant in the woods, covering by hand and not depending upon Nature to do the work.

Sometimes people ask me to supply them with seed which they may scatter through the woods and fields. This is a wasteful and profitless method. Broadcasting seed in the fields will usually result only in those of the weediest nature germinating and growing. Wherever it is sown the soil should be raked and stirred and then the seed covered. Remember that Nature has to depend upon hard rains, insects, rodents and birds for distributing and covering her seed, and that if one in a thousand which is produced by the wildflowers and trees should germinate and grow, the human race would be crowded off the earth.

After germination the young plants should be protected against driving rains, rodents and drouth.

Strong growing species, such as Lilies and Jack-in-the-pulpit, may be left in the beds until they have reached such size that they may be safely planted into their permanent home, but smaller growing plants, such as Gentian and Bluebells of Scotland, are best transplanted into small pots or flats as soon as they attain sufficient size. They may then be given the care which their delicate nature at this age requires, and as they grow they may be transplanted into larger pots, cold frames or to their permanent home.

PROPAGATION BY CUTTINGS. Many wildflowers vary greatly in different plants of the same species. They may vary in color, in season of blossoming, in height or habit of growth, or the size and form of the flower itself. Now if seed is sown from individual plants of a species which varies in this manner there is no assurance that more than a small percentage, if any, of the resulting seedlings will be identical with the plant from which the seed was saved.

Examples of this kind are the white Phlox divaricata, Butterflyweed, White Fringed Polygala, Hepaticas and pink forms of Trailing Arbutus. To increase the supply of these plants one must resort to other methods of propagation than growing from seed.

The common method of effecting an increase in these plants is to grow them from cuttings, either root cuttings or softwood cuttings of the top. For cuttings such as Arbutus or Twinflower a mixture of half sand and half ground peat is desirable, never permitting this soil mixture to dry out until the cuttings have struck root and are well established.

Root cuttings are made by cutting the roots into pieces two or three inches long and burying them in moist sand to which some leafmold and soil have been added. These cuttings may be started in the winter in a greenhouse or in early spring before top growth has begun.

Some of the plants which respond readily to this method of propagating are Anemones, Butterflyweed, Shootingstar, Mountain Phlox and Flowering Spurge. When either root or top cuttings become established on their own roots they may be transplanted and treated the same as seedlings.

PROPAGATION BY LAYERING. The class of wildflowers known as ground covers have the habit of sending out runners which produce roots along the stem as they travel. In growing these plants under cultivation this rooting process may be hastened by covering the runners at intervals with soil. This method is known as layering and pieces of the runner with roots attached may be transplanted to form new plants. This method of propagation is particularly adapted to Partridgeberry, Twinflower, Creeping Snowberry, Moneywort and Blue Myrtle.

PROPAGATION BY DIVISION. The method of propagating most widely practiced next to growing from seed is division of the clumps. These clumps may have been increased naturally by creeping root stalks, as with the Barren Strawberry, or an increase in the number of the buds to the plants, as with the Cypripediums, or simply a natural increase in the size of the clumps, as with the Phlox.

These species may be divided with least shock to the plant when they are dormant, either in late summer or fall or in very early spring. Early fall is perhaps the time to be preferred, as many species will become rerooted before winter sets in. It is well to give them protection for the first winter, at least, so that the frost will not throw them out on the ground in the spring.

The four methods of propagating described are all the ordinary wildflower grower will be interested in, for some kinds of plants may be increased in number by two or more methods. The Partridgeberry, for instance, may be increased by all four methods described. And sometimes which proves to be the best may depend upon the person rather than the plant.

It is impossible for me to give any fixed rules for one to follow, owing to extremely variable local conditions. Then again, as I said at the beginning of this book, one may follow certain methods for several years, attributing success to certain practices only to find out later that success was due to some reason entirely foreign to what he had attributed it.

But, however you undertake to propagate the wildflowers, remember that you are doing pioneer work and may reason out or stumble onto facts which will be of tremendous value to the horticultural world.

PLANTING. Unless I have specifically given the time for planting different species, the reader may assume that they transplant well in either autumn or early spring. Varieties that start into growth in very early spring are preferably planted in autumn. Wildflowers of this nature include Dutchmans-breeches, Springbeauty and Troutlilies. Plants, like Mertensia, which complete their growth in midsummer, will become more firmly established and give best results the following season if moved in late July and August.

The depth to which they should be set depends upon the nature of the plant. Those which grow from buds or eyes, like Ladyslippers, Clintonia and Hepaticas, should be planted so that the buds are not much below the surface of the soil.

Plants growing from a bulb, like the Springbeauty, Wild Bean and Lilies, may be planted to a much greater depth. Probably four times the depth of the bulb itself is a fair rule to go by. The wild Iris, of course, should be planted with the rhizome practically at the surface of the ground.

Many wildflowers, such as Phlox, Asters, Sunflowers and Trilliums, are most beautiful when planted in clumps or masses. Other plants, such as Cardinalflower, Thermopsis, Fringe-orchids, Gayfeathers and Lilies are more satisfactory if the plants are permitted to develop their full individual beauty by being planted singly or in small groups.

WINTER PROTECTION. In protecting plants for the winter I find nothing better than dead leaves. If covered before cold weather with four or five inches of leaves the soil will usually come through our severe northern winters without freezing much. But be sure to remove the leaves in the spring before they smother the young plants. Do not take them off all at once, and a few may be left to rot into the soil.

Evergreen boughs afford very good protection, but the needles fall from these boughs in spring before it is safe to remove them, thus making the soil much more acid.

INDOOR WILDFLOWERS. No one likes wildflowers better than a shut-in. At no season of the year are they worth more for keeping up one's courage than in late winter and there are so many species that may be grown successfully indoors that they may well be used more for this purpose.

All native plants of the temperate climate require a cool dormant season even if it does freeze. They will not thrive unless they have it, so if one plans to force them into blossom out of their natural season it is necessary to give them a reasonable dormant season before starting them.

For practical purposes the average person will not care to have them come into bloom before winter. The way to handle them for this purpose is to pack them in soil in late fall and leave them in a shed or even out-of-doors until they have had a season of cold weather. After winter sets in, in December, these native plants may be brought into the cellar, thawed out gradually and planted out in pots, flats, terrariums, or indoor windowboxes, just as one would plant them out-of-doors in springtime.

They should not have too much sun to start with, but give them a chance to get their roots established before forcing them too much. In the case of those with fleshy roots, like the Mertensia, it is well to leave them in the dark until they have become rooted and started to grow a little.

The time required to bring these various wildflowers into bloom will vary from two weeks with Hepaticas to two months with some of the Ladyslippers, depending upon the temperature. After they have finished blossoming they may be kept until spring and then transplanted into the open. Of course they will not bloom again this same year, and many species will become dormant much earlier than they naturally would. If one wishes to force the rarer species I hope that he will make arrangements for planting them out-of-doors after forcing.

There are many species which are so readily propagated that one should have no qualms in forcing them for the benefit of an invalid or anyone else, even though they are not saved for out-of-door planting. Among these common, easily grown plants I would include Jack-in-the-pulpit, Wild Marshmarigold, Springbeauty, Squirrelcorn, Dutchmans-breeches, White Troutlily, Mertensia, Mitrewort, Foamflower, Bloodroot, Quaker Ladies, Early Saxifrage, Windflower, Little Merrybells and Violets.

Among the rarer plants which force readily indoors are Wild Ginger, Calypso, Ladyslippers, Trailing Arbutus, Shootingstar, Hepaticas, Crested Iris, Twinleaf, Showy Orchis, Rattlesnake Plantain.

PLANT ENEMIES. Wildflowers have many natural enemies. The worst of these is fire, which every year destroys numberless millions, but even a good fire is appreciated by the Fireweeds and Pokeberry.

Another natural enemy is the thoughtless human being, who collects them at the wrong time of year or in the wrong manner. The gatherer of some wildflowers, such as the Wild Columbine, is, however, benefiting the plant from which he picks a blossom because plants of this nature become much stronger and more vigorous if not allowed to make seed. Plants which are naturally biennials become perennials if not permitted to make seed.

A grower of the American Lotus tells me the greatest expense in growing it successfully is in removing a large percentage of the roots each season. As the Lotus seeds freely if the blossoms are not picked, the bottom of the pool or pond soon becomes so filled with masses of roots that it does not bloom well. I have seen small ponds where this was also true of our common White Waterlily. Yet, in spite of this fact, I believe that one middlewestern state has a law which prohibits the picking of Lotus blossoms.

The collectors of roots and herbs for wholesale druggists have reduced many species to a minimum, but the fact that the Ginseng still persists in about its usual quantity shows how hard it is to really exterminate a species.

In the Middle West draining the bogs to make arable land has come close to exterminating the White Ladyslipper (Cypripedium candidum).

Other natural enemies of wildflowers are insect and larger wild animal life. The wild deer are particularly fond of Lily buds, and as I write this, all that remains of two beds containing several hundred plants of Gray's Lily and Meadow Lily is a single bud on one of the Gray's Lilies, and telltale hoof prints on each bed prove that the wild deer have had at least one good feast this summer. I expect the bulbs will be stronger for having the buds removed, so I am not disappointed, but when one grows them for the flowers an act like this on the part of the deer is not appreciated.

The wild deer are not the only wood folks that like Lilies, for Peter Rabbit is equally fond of them. He will also go out of his way to eat the tops of the Twistedstalks. Peter's work can be detected from the fact that he makes a clean cut such as would be made with a sharp knife, while the work of other animals is more ragged.

Johnny Chuck thinks that the Spiderwort was grown especially for him, and he also likes Phlox in variety and many other plants.

One of the most aggravating of neighbors is Jerry Muskrat. If Jerry would confine his menu to Cattails and Lotus roots we could not criticise him too much, but when, for variety, he takes home to his family a newly planted clump of Arrowhead, White Waterlily, Cardinal-flower or some other choice species, and then digs a hole in the dam letting half the water out of the pond, he gets himself put into the pest class, and is very far from being a desirable neighbor.

The little pests are always with us. Even the tiny ants will steal the seeds of the Arbutus just as they ripen. Maybe they do not call it stealing. Probably they are obeying the strongest law in the world— the law of self-preservation.

So let me say—or is it necessary to say?—that eternal vigilance is the price of successfully growing wildflowers even though cultural directions and soil requirements for the species are definitely known.

CHAPTER V

The Ladyslippers

⇒》⇒》《⇐《⇐

THE Ladyslippers are our most romantic family, for thinking of them takes one far into the northwoods, the country of romance and adventure, and helps one to live in his imagination the lives of the earliest French voyageurs and adventurers, for the Ladyslippers, with the exception of the Pink Moccasin Flower (Cypripedium acaule) and the White Ladyslipper (Cypripedium candidum), abhor civilization and seek the deep recesses of the hardwoods forest and cedar swamp.

Strangely enough, the common Pink Moccasin Flower, which in New England grows abundantly in the pine barrens close to our larger cities, is really the most difficult to grow successfully when moved from its native element. For several years I have been growing eight species of Ladyslippers, seven of them successfully, and one of them, California Ladyslipper (Cypripedium californicum), with only partial success, for it seems to die of homesickness after a year or two in our New England climate.

The only sure way to propagate our Ladyslippers successfully is by division. It is true Nature increases their number by seed, but, as far as I know, man has not successfully accomplished this yet, and whoever discovers how to grow our native Cypripediums readily from seed will be doing a rich service to the horticultural world. Most of them may be divided every two or three years and increase about as rapidly as peonies. Do not plant them too deeply because if you do the crowns will rot away. Set them just below the surface of the ground, as you would a peony, and never put them where the crowns will be covered with water. The varieties that grow in the bogs are never planted by Nature where water will stand over them, but are always put on hummocks where the roots can go down deeply and draw the plentiful amount of moisture which they require.

17

SHOWY LADYSLIPPER
Cypripedium reginae
(formerly *Cypripedium spectabile*)

Fall or early spring is the best time to plant Ladyslippers, for the new buds are fully developed at this time. Nevertheless, most any of these plants may be moved at any time during the year if a ball of earth is taken with them. For winter protection a light mulch of leaves is the best that can be given, but I do not find it really necessary to protect them at all.

RAMSHEAD LADYSLIPPER (Cypripedium arietinum) is the earliest of all to blossom. This variety is not a robust grower. It is a native of northern Vermont and New York and found sparingly elsewhere, sometimes on hummocks in the cedar bogs or sometimes growing in the thick moss on the ledges. It is not at all difficult to handle. It grows about eight to ten inches tall and its small flowers of red and white are shaped so grotesquely that someone imagined they resembled a ram's head, but to me they look more like the head of a common housefly. May heaven help the lady unfortunate enough to have feet shaped like these slippers!

PINK MOCCASIN FLOWER (Cypripedium acaule) is found growing very generally in the thick leafmold of our mountains and also in the thin, poorer soil under the pines in southeastern New England. It sends its blossom stem with a single large rose pink flower to a height of ten to fifteen inches from a pair of dark green basal leaves and blossoms about the last of May, in Vermont, before the Ramshead Ladyslipper has finished blooming.

This is a variety which will not tolerate alkali, but insists upon acid soil if it is to thrive. While it grows in drier locations than the other Ladyslippers, yet when it is planted it must not be allowed to dry out until it has become established. Covering with a mulch of pine needles is a help in this respect. Our southern and western friends seem to have difficulty in making the Cypripedium acaule live more than one or two years and I have often heard it spoken of as a biennial, but when one realizes that the plant does not attain blooming size until the third year from seed, the biennial theory receives a severe jolt. It is more likely the heat of the longer summer season or lack of sufficient acid in the soil that makes the Pink Moccasin Flower so short lived when taken away from its northern home.

WHITE MOCCASIN FLOWER (Cypripedium acaule alba) has a much more northern range than the pink one and in some sections of northern New England, New York and Canada is nearly as plentiful.

Its cultural requirements are the same.   A well-grown clump of the exquisitely beautiful White Moccasin Flower is a delightful picture.

WHITE LADYSLIPPER (Cypripedium candidum) has very little in common with the Moccasin Flower.   It is a native of the marl bogs of Ohio and Michigan, growing in the open sun and is the only member of its family to insist on alkaline conditions.   This little white slipper has become very rare on account of the swamps being drained for agricultural purposes, but fortunately it increases rapidly under cultivation, at least doubling the number of buds to the clump each year.   An old clump of this species may have as many as fifty or sixty flower stems, and sometime, through commercial cultivation, it may become plentiful again.   Cypripedium candidum attains a height of one foot.

MOUNTAIN LADYSLIPPER (Cypripedium montanum), from the western mountains, is somewhat similar to candidum in growth, but this species has pink markings instead of being pure white.   We grow it successfully in a neutral soil.

COMMON YELLOW LADYSLIPPER (Cypripedium pubescens). Here is a chance for an argument.   Is there one or two species?   Some grow Cypripedium pubescens and some grow Cypripedium parviflorum and some have both.   For the time being it is my opinion that they are all one species, but with a wide variation among the individual plants. I expect many will heartily disagree with me as to this, but whatever you call it, the Yellow Ladyslipper is one of the easiest to grow, taking kindly to ordinary perennial garden conditions.   As it grows wild in the woods or on the hummocks in the swamps one finds a considerable mixture of clay in the soil, more so than is found where other Ladyslippers grow.

Professor Robert T. Jackson of Peterborough, New Hampshire, has a plant of the Yellow Ladyslipper which has been growing in his garden for over fifty years, and when I saw it a few years ago it had practically as many blossom stalks as it was years old.   The season of blooming is late May or early June in New England.   The stems sometimes, though rarely, reach a height of eighteen inches.   The Yellow Ladyslipper also has the quality of fragrance, such an intense, sweetish fragrance as to be almost nauseating.

CALIFORNIA LADYSLIPPER (Cypripedium californicum).   Perhaps one should not advertise his failures, but the California Ladyslipper, which produces several small white slippers with yellow laces on each stalk, is really worth trying to grow, and some day we shall find a reason for our failure with it.   The plants which we secure from the West are pretty sure to blossom the spring after being planted.   They are fairly sure to live another year, but about the third year they give up the ghost and we have to renew them.

SHOWY LADYSLIPPER (Cypripedium spectabile) is a giant of the northwoods, growing in the dense recesses of the forest and on hummocks in the bogs.   The blossoming stalks reach a height of two to two and a half feet and the large clumps present an almost tropical appearance in a country far removed from the tropics.   The Showy Ladyslipper with its large flowers of pink and white may be readily grown in the garden where the soil is moist and there is partial shade. But here again let me caution you, do not plant them where it is too wet.   If in doubt, it is better to err on the side of dryness.   The blooming season of the Showy Ladyslipper is late June.

Flower, side view.

Flower, front view.

RAGGED FRINGE-ORCHID
Habenaria lacera

CHAPTER VI

The Fringe-Orchids

≫≫≫ ≪≪

THE Habenarias or Fringe-orchids are native in a great many species, but less than a dozen are well known. All require plenty of moisture if they are to do their best. Full or partial shade is also necessary for all of the kinds that I shall mention with the exception of the Ragged Fringe-orchid (Habenaria lacera). They are quite easily transplanted into the wildflower garden if they can be given plenty of rich black soil in which to grow, and their spikes of midsummer color are a delightful attraction.

Nature propagates Fringe-orchids by seed, but the wildflower enthusiasts will have to depend on offshoots from the mother plant to increase his supply, and even then I fear it will not increase very rapidly. But if conditions are right Nature may take a hand and assist in increasing the supply from self-sown seed. Like the Ladyslippers, the Fringe-orchids do not take kindly to the efforts of man to increase them from seed.

RAGGED FRINGE-ORCHID (Habenaria lacera) is the best known member of the family, being found plentifully in the moist upland pastures and meadows of New England. Its greenish yellow flower spikes, which grow to a height of about a foot, would not attract much attention except for the very ragged edges of the individual blossoms, which look as if someone had spent a great deal of time upon them with a pair of tiny scissors.

YELLOW FRINGE-ORCHID (Habenaria ciliaris) is mentioned in some old books as being a native of Vermont. As a matter of fact I know of no place where it grows wild in New England, although, of course, there may be many. The supply of plants comes largely from the South. Our success with this variety has not been as satisfactory as one might hope for, but the strikingly gorgeous orange-colored flower spikes on twelve inch stems make it worth every effort to try to handle it successfully in captivity. Some day we shall have better success than we have had so far.

LARGE PURPLE FRINGE-ORCHID (Habenaria fimbriata). Whoever has traveled the highways and trails of the Green Mountains in mid-July has certainly become acquainted with this Habenaria, for it is very abundant in the swamps and along the roadsides at an elevation of two thousand feet or more, but it is also easily transplanted, making itself at home in good rich garden soil, preferably in partial shade. The beautiful, orchid-colored flowers are borne on stalks one to two feet tall, and in addition to being pleasing to the eye, possess a strangely exotic and seductive fragrance not found in many New England wildflowers.

SMALL PURPLE FRINGE-ORCHID (Habenaria psycodes). Many have difficulty in distinguishing the Small Purple Fringe-orchid from its larger relative. There is really not so much difference in the size of the blossoms as the names would indicate, but the Habenaria fimbriata blossoms two to three weeks earlier than Habenaria psycodes and is deeper in color. Besides, the Small Purple Fringe-orchid does not possess the delightful, elusive fragrance of its mountain relative. Then, too, Habenaria psycodes is nearly always found at a much lower elevation. It is an inhabitant of the wet swamps, and does its best in quite dense shade.

WHITE FRINGE-ORCHID (Habenaria blephariglottis) is a beautiful tall white-flowering Habenaria found around the edges of the higher mountain ponds and lakes, usually growing very near the water, and sometimes where the water actually does lie around the roots. It is not so plentiful, nor does it grow so readily, as its purple brothers.

WHITE BOG-ORCHID (Habernaria dilatata) grows in the same locality as blephariglottis, but does not attain such a large size.

HOOKER ORCHID (Habenaria hookeri) is a plant of different habits than the foregoing Fringe-orchids, growing sometimes under spruce and balsam trees and again in dense hardwoods shade surrounded by Moccasin Flowers, Clintonia, Bunchberries and Painted Trilliums, indicating quite clearly that it prefers acid soil conditions. The two large glossy green basal leaves four inches in diameter lie flat upon the ground and the flower stalk, bearing greenish-yellow blossoms, rises to a height of twelve to fifteen inches. It is not common except at an elevation exceeding two thousand feet.

LARGE ROUNDLEAVED ORCHID (Habenaria orbiculata) is of growth similar to the Hooker Orchid, but is found at lower elevations in the woods of beech, birch and maple, where soil conditions are not so acid. The large basal leaves are not so dark green and the blossoms are nearly white instead of green in color. It is a rare and beautiful member of the Orchid family.

ROSE POGONIA
Pogonia ophioglossoides

AMERICAN CRANBERRY
Vaccinium macrocarpon

CHAPTER VII
Little Bog Orchids

-»»-»»-««-««-

THE Orchid family offers a decided contrast in comparing the big Showy Ladyslipper with its tiny relatives of the bogs, but what these little bog Orchids lack in size they make up by their countless numbers. As far as I know, no one has seriously attempted to propagate these little species commercially because they grow in such limitless quantities when one finds them at all, and they are so easily transplanted that the efforts of wildflower propagators have been turned in more necessary directions.

Although these tiny Orchids, which I shall describe, grow naturally in very wet meadows and swamps, yet they move easily and safely to any good moist garden spot, although I would protect them for the winter. One might think the plants which grow almost in the water would be very hardy, but as a matter of fact, the bogs seldom freeze except for the hummocks.

ROSE POGONIA (Pogonia ophioglossoides) grows only about six inches tall and has grasslike foliage. Whoever first called it by the common name of Snakemouth may have been justified according to the shape of the flower, but he certainly should have known better than to let a name like this ever be applied to such a beautiful little plant. It carpets some of our mountain swamps and the banks of small streams with thousands of shimmering pink blossoms in early July. Some folks say the color is lavender-pink, but it requires very close examination to discern the lavender. It grows in open sun and bears one blossom to the stalk. Plant the roots of Pogonia about two inches below the surface.

GRASS-PINK ORCHID (Calopogon pulchellus). This dainty little bog Orchid grows under similar conditions to the Pogonia, but from a small white bulb instead of a root. The flowers are more nearly purple in color and several are borne on a stalk. The bulb should be planted about three inches below the surface of the ground. It is easily grown,

27

but unfortunately the foliage is so slender that it is often mistaken for grass and weeded out when planted in the garden. Calopogon blossoms in June and July on stalks slightly taller than those of the Pogonia.

ARETHUSA (Arethusa bulbosa). In the bogs and meadows of eastern North America, the dainty and beautiful rose pink yawning flowers are found on six to ten inch stems in May and June. The Arethusa grows from a small white bulb.

CALYPSO (Calypso bulbosa). Calypso is one of our more elusive wildflowers, particularly as it can hide in a pretty small corner, even on a rotten log, or in a niche in the moist, shaded ledges. Although found occasionally in the East the principal source of supply is the far western mountains.

The little bulb with a single green leaf attached should be planted in autumn in moss or debris rather than soil. This single leaf, nearly as broad as it is long, remains green all winter and in early spring the little blossom stalks get adventurous and rise nobly to a height of two to three inches and then unfold one of the most grotesquely beautiful wildflowers. It seems to try to overcome the terrible malformation of its flowers with exquisitely beautiful coloring. They seem like gnomes of the wood. Perhaps they are ashamed of their grotesqueness, which causes them to hide from civilization. After flowering, the green leaf dies down and a new bulb is formed which in turn will send up another leaf the coming fall.

CHAPTER VIII
Other Orchids

->>> ->>> <<<- <<<-

SO extensive is the Orchid family that several books might be written about this family alone and I shall discuss only a few more of the common and attractive species native to Northeastern United States. Members of this family grow under such varying conditions as the dry pine barrens and the swamps, from the high mountain tops to sea level and from the densest shade to the sunniest fields.

SHOWY ORCHIS (Orchis spectabilis) is one of the choicest species of springtime. It is found in the hardwoods shade where the soil is neutral or even slightly alkaline and often where it is composed of disintegrated slate stone and leafmold. This delightful little Orchid, whose flower stem grows about six inches tall from a pair of glaucous green leaves which, late in the season, lie flat on the ground, is lavender and white in color and is one of the more fragrant members of its family. If conditions are right, the Showy Orchis will double in number each year. Before it rots away the mother root produces two offshoots, a large one on one side and a small one on the other. Perhaps someone knows why these two offshoots are not equal in size, but Nature probably has a reason for it. Showy Orchis enjoys as companions the Maidenhair Fern, Sharplobe Hepatica, Bloodroot and Wood Violets.

NODDING LADIES-TRESSES (Spiranthes cernua). Returning to the marshes for more Orchids we find the Ladies-tresses, which blossoms in August and September with eight to fifteen inch twisted spikes of white, fragrant flowers. It is easily transplanted and thrives best among the grass in the moist meadows. For a companion it is quite partial to the Fringed Gentian.

Another variety is the Wide-leaved Ladies-tresses (Spiranthes plantagineum). It is of similar growth, but blossoms in early summer. It grows to a height of ten inches, is less fragrant and has wider leaves.

LILY TWAYBLADE (Liparis lilifolia). Despite the fact that one author says this is found on dry shaded hillsides, I must say that I have usually found it growing on hummocks in the bogs. The little loose racemes of flowers on six inch stems have such a phantom airiness that except for the delicate orchid or yellowish coloring they would look like almost nothing at all. As it is, they are most attractively fragile.

LOESEL TWAYBLADE (Liparis loeseli). I find this growing wild in company with Lily Twayblade. It is just a little larger and has flowers of yellowish green. Both blossom in June.

DOWNY RATTLESNAKE PLANTAIN (Goodyera pubescens). The other members of the Orchid family certainly left the Goodyeras high and dry, and we find them growing in the dry soil under pine trees. Their beauty is in the veining of the leaves. The Rattlesnake Plantain has foot tall spikes of white flowers in August and distinctly marked, white-veined, nearly prostrate leaves, which make it attractive the year around.

CREEPING RATTLESNAKE PLANTAIN (Goodyera repens var. ophioides) is the less common and more prostrate form of Goodyera and is found more in the northern hardwoods than it is under the pines. It spreads rapidly from creeping root stalks and a single plant may form a considerable colony in a few years. The veining is not so white and conspicuous as the veining of the Goodyera pubescens.

CHAPTER IX

Trailing Arbutus *Epigaea repens*

PERHAPS more people have failed in trying to grow the Trailing Arbutus than with any other North American wildflower. These failures have been due largely to the fact that they have used wild or collected plants of such size that failure was practically inevitable.

The nature of the Trailing Arbutus is such that its creeping stems form a carpet on the ground, in maturity as much as two to three feet across, and so many have taken up a portion of this carpet, failing to secure the root of the plant itself. If wild plants must be used it is unwise to move those more than six inches in diameter.

However, it is wholly unnecessary and undesirable to transplant Arbutus from the wild. In transplanting thousands of young nursery grown plants each year I have no heavier loss with them than with Violets or other common plants.

The Trailing Arbutus may be grown either from seed or from cuttings. After the plant blossoms in early May, if weather conditions have been right for pollenizing them, small round seed pods will form in clusters of three to six or eight and continue to develop until by the middle of June they attain the size of a pea. Then it is necessary to watch them very carefully. Not only are chipmunks, ants and bugs very fond of them, but the pods are likely to pop open and distribute their tiny seeds without any notice. So, just as soon as one finds the seeds are turning brown, even though the pod itself is still green, it is time to gather them. They should be sown in a mixture of sand and acid leafmold immediately, and in from three to six weeks will germinate freely, attaining a diameter of about half an inch the first season. If grown in a greenhouse they may be transplanted into pots or flats at any time. If grown out-of-doors it is better to leave them until the following spring.

Trailing Arbutus
Epigaea repens

Twinflower
Linnaea borealis

The second year, if well cared for, they will make plants two inches or more across and the third year grow to blossoming size.

If one wishes to grow Arbutus of a certain shade of color, it is necessary to grow them from cuttings, as the seed cannot be depended upon to come true. These cuttings should be made soon after the plants finish blossoming, using the ends of the runners and removing any seed pods there may be on them. They should be three to six inches in length and set in a mixture of half sand and half granulated peat. If not permitted to dry out at all they will become well rooted by fall, often blossoming the year after the cutting is taken. This is a much more rapid method of propagating than growing them from seed and if one has sufficient stock to get the cuttings from will prove more profitable commercially.

Trailing Arbutus has one prime requirement. The soil must be very acid. It grows wild in company with Wood Lily and Lowbush Blueberry. Some claim that if the soil is acid it can be successfully grown anywhere, but I cannot agree with this. It does grow better in shade than in full sun, and if planted where it is too hot and dry is likely to be short-lived.

In transplanting we invariably move it with a ball of earth, the size of the ball depending upon the size of the plant, and if the newly moved plants are in sun or only partial shade a mulch of pine needles is very beneficial to help hold the moisture and keep the leaves from burning. It is our practice to cover them so that one can just see the plants through the needles.

The Trailing Arbutus responds quickly to fertilization. If the soil is very acid, manure water will give good results, although it is alkaline. But if the soil is not very acid a light application of sulphate of ammonia in early summer will help the plants to grow stronger and with better color to their leaves.

To the folks who wish to grow Arbutus, but have no acid soil, I would suggest that they apply aluminum sulphate at the rate of half a pound to the square yard of surface. Oak leafmold and pine needles worked into the soil will also make it acid. Even sawdust from conifers will sometimes suffice. Do not let the plants dry out until they have become thoroughly established and even then, although they grow wild in seemingly dry locations, they appreciate water so long as it does not stand around them.

DOWNY YELLOW VIOLET
Viola pubescens

CHAPTER X

Violets

ACCORDING to the Bulletin No. 224 written by Ezra Brainard and published by the Vermont Agricultural Experiment Station, there are seventy-five species of North American Violets found north of Mexico, and when we consider that many of them hybridize freely one can imagine the difficulty which an amateur might experience in trying to identify the different plants which he finds. In my own work of propagating wildflowers I have used only about a dozen species, principally those native to eastern North America.

Several kinds of Violets have what botanists call cleistogamous blossoms. These are flowers which follow the early, showy colored flowers of the plant and which are produced on very short scapes hidden beneath the leaves and sometimes in the soil itself. These flowers have no petals and they never open. They contain very little pollen, but as it is confined wholly within the blossom the seeds are invariably fertile. Common species of Violets producing flowers which are cleistogamous are Roundleaf Violet, Birdsfoot Violet, Palm Violet and the Blue Marsh Violet.

All kinds of Violets can be propagated from seed and many kinds by division of the plant. In favorable locations certain species, particularly the Blue Marsh Violet in the garden and the Sweet White Violet in the woodland, may have a tendency to become obnoxious, as they seed freely and grow so rapidly that more fragile flowers may become half smothered by them.

BIRDSFOOT VIOLET (Viola pedata) is the most common native species in cultivation. Although not so strong a grower as some of the others, Birdsfoot Violet is common in dry, sandy soil and open woods from southern New England to the Gulf of Mexico. It makes a neat, compact plant of beautiful, dissected foliage about three inches tall, covered in late May and early June with large, light blue flowers an inch or more across.

TWO-COLORED BIRDSFOOT VIOLET (Viola pedata bicolor) is a more delicate form with upper petals of pale blue and lower ones rich royal purple, making it probably the showiest of all Violets. Occasionally a pure white blossom of the Birdsfoot is found. These Violets take very kindly to naturalizing and grow in almost any location, sun or shade, so long as the soil is not too wet.

BUTTERFLY VIOLET (Viola papilionacea) is the small, light blue field Violet found carpeting the open pastures and hillsides in early spring and blossoming occasionally again in the autumn.

BLUE MARSH VIOLET (Viola cucullata) is the Long Stemmed Violet of the swamps, but when brought into the garden or in drier land it grows heavily to foliage and the blossoms seem to grow larger and on shorter stems. The masses of green leaves, which Viola cucullata produces throughout the summer, make it very satisfactory as a ground cover in certain places, but those places should not be where more delicate plants are growing.

PALM VIOLET (Viola palmata). It gets its name from the shape of its leaves. It has the heaviest foliage of any Violet I have grown, the plants making large, substantial clumps a foot in height and completely covering the ground in moist or fairly dry shade. It makes a very satisfactory ground cover for waste places. The pale blue flowers are nearly an inch across, but as the flower stems grow about the same height as the leaves the blossoms are not so conspicuous as those of the Birdsfoot Violet.

ROUNDLEAF VIOLET (Viola rotundifolia) is one of the earliest wildflowers to bloom, the tiny, bright yellow flowers on one to three inch stems blossoming while there is still snow in the woods. One would hardly connect this tiny yellow flower with its large, roundish leaves three to four inches across, which carpet the ground in late summer. Viola rotundifolia is propagated from seed produced by cleistogamous flowers in late fall, which peculiarity caused it to be regarded as two species by early botanists.

DOWNY YELLOW VIOLET (Viola pubescens) is a foot tall northern species of yellow Violet, which blossoms in late May. It grows in the rich woods or along old stone walls and roadsides. The common name is due to the fact that the underside of the leaves is covered with a whitish down.

SWEET WHITE VIOLET (Viola blanda) is usually found growing in the moist woods and bogs. It multiplies rapidly from seed and short runners and if given an opportunity will overrun less robust and prolific sorts. Nevertheless, it is a most beautiful little wildflower.

CANADA VIOLET (Viola canadensis) is a true northern Violet always found in the rich deciduous woods of the mountains. It grows a foot or more tall. The fragrant flowers are white with a purplish tinge. This Violet blossoms more or less throughout the summer and fall.

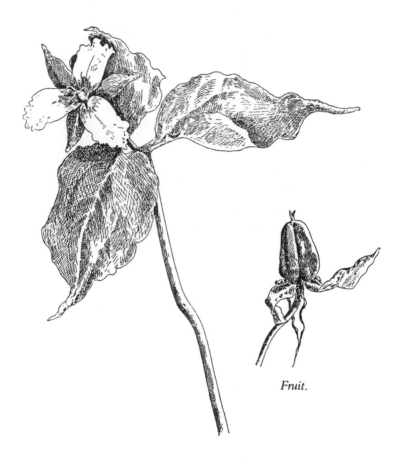

Fruit.

PAINTED TRILLIUM
Trillium undulatum

CHAPTER XI

Two Months of Trilliums

->>> ->>> <<<- <<<-

IN the days of some years ago, when the author was at the right age to make the life of his district school teacher anything but a lot of perpetual happiness, the departing snows of spring invariably brought a series of adventures. First, of course, was the adventure of going swimming in the icy waters of the melting snow and getting put to bed for it if found out. Then there was the adventure of finding the first frogs' eggs and the different uses that could be made of them; the attempts at drowning woodchucks out of their holes (which resulted in a hundred per cent failure), and another adventure in which I was usually successful—that of finding the first wildflower to blossom.

Sometimes it would be the Hepatica and sometimes the little Yellow Violet, but, much as I wish to champion our New England wildflowers, I must say that since I have been growing the North American plants commercially neither the Yellow Violet nor the Hepatica can any longer lay claim to being the earliest to bloom. They have to surrender this honor to a mild-mannered little fellow from the Middle West, the Dwarf Trillium.

For a beginner in growing wildflowers there is hardly a family more satisfactory than the Trilliums. They grow wonderfully well in hardwoods shade and rejoice in a plentiful supply of leafmold. All may be propagated from seed, although it requires two years to germinate and two or three more before they get large enough to blossom. Some, like the Snow Trillium and California Trillium, propagate most readily from division, and when established, a bed will increase of its own accord. I think the best time to plant them is in early autumn, planting to a depth of about four times the diameter of the root and covering them with a light mulch of leaves for the first winter.

DWARF TRILLIUM (Trillium nivale). This little plant, shy and good-natured, can hardly wait for the snows to disappear before sticking his little head up to a height of about four inches and unfolding a lovely pure white flower, in size resembling a large Hepatica or small Bloodroot blossom more than a Trillium, but indisputably the first to bloom.

Trillium nivale has a dwarf relative from the Pacific coast, called Trillium rivale. Trillium rivale, however, is pink and does not seem to blossom so freely here in the East. It may be due to getting smaller bulbs, or perhaps it spends so much time bragging about the wonderful California climate it came from that it forgets to get busy and grow. This, however, cannot be said about

CALIFORNIA TRILLIUM (Trillium sessile californicum), which is a giant stemless species. I do not mean that the plant is stemless, but the flower itself is stemless, sitting right on the leaves. It is perfectly at home here in the East, and bears large white blossoms about the middle of May.

PURPLE TRILLIUM (Trillium erectum). The earliest eastern Trillium to blossom is Trillium erectum, which poets delight to call Wakerobin, but which the small boys of the local country schools call Bloody Benjamin. It is a lusty grower to a height of twelve to fifteen inches with flowers that are ox blood in color. Its fragrance might be called an odor. I think the Trillium erectum, growing in company with its friends, the Maidenhair Fern, Bloodroot, Wild Oats and Wild Ginger, is one of our nicest eastern wildflowers.

SNOW TRILLIUM (Trillium grandiflorum), which grows extensively through the entire length of the Appalachians, has been literally planted by the million. It propagates very readily, and appreciates any extra attention that may be given it until the blossoms may develop to a diameter of three or four inches. Large, well-established colonies are a beautiful sight indeed. Bulbs may be obtained cheaply and will succeed under any reasonable conditions where the soil is not too acid.

As the flowers of the Snow Trillium age they turn first pale pink and then almost light red in color, and innumerable amateurs think that they have discovered a new species when they find the aging blossoms of this species.

There is also a variety of this Trillium with a broad green band the length of each petal, which gives it a very distinctive appearance. It is not at all common.

PRAIRIE TRILLIUM (Trillium recurvatum) is a stemless variety and its beauty lies in its mottled leaves rather than its brown flowers, which never completely open. The recurved sepals give it its name. While native of the Central and Southern States, yet it is very easily grown here in the North and every plant is practically sure to blossom in late May.

PAINTED TRILLIUM (Trillium undulatum) is apparently estranged from the rest of the family because it likes a different location and insists on growing in very acid soil along with Bunchberry, Trailing Arbutus and the Pink Moccasin Flower. It is a late May bloomer, not quite so large as the Wakerobin. Its flowers have a red center and white petals striped with red, like peppermint candy sticks. Although the other Trilliums have showy seed pods in August, yet the fruit of the Painted Trillium is the most striking of all, being intensely red and enlivening a drab season with its brilliant color.

YELLOW TRILLIUM (Trillium flavum) does not seem to be classified by our botanists. Our plants of this variety were sent to me by Mrs. Wight of Tennessee, who tells me that it is very prevalent on one mountain there. It is a strong grower with mottled leaves and pale yellow flowers about the color of Flavescens Iris.

ROSE TRILLIUM (Trillium stylosum) is the latest of them all. It is a pale pink variety from the South, not so free to blossom as some. It is not quite so strong a grower in the North, but nevertheless is fairly reliable and very much worthwhile and extends the season of Trilliums to approximately sixty days' blooming period.

NODDING TRILLIUM (Trillium cernuum) is a northern white Trillium similar to the Snow Trillium except that it is somewhat smaller and the blossom is nodding instead of erect.

Besides the Trilliums which I have mentioned there are sports and hybrids among the different species, and there is an opportunity for one to do much work with them.

42

AMERICAN WOOD ANEMONE
Anemone quinquefolia

RUE ANEMONE
Anemonella thalictroides

CHAPTER XII

Along the Woodland Pathway

H ERE is an opportunity for surprise planting, for if one follows the woodland pathway in its meandering through thickets of witch-hazel and alder and across tiny streams one never knows what the next turn will bring forth. While most of our woodland flowers grow in the hardwoods under beeches and maples, oaks and other deciduous trees, there are several kinds which seem to do best under the conifers. Among these are the Pink Moccasin Flower and Rattlesnake Plantain discussed in other chapters.

Ideal plants for woodlands described elsewhere include the Columbines, Aralias, all of the Plants with Bright Berries, many kinds of Asters and Orchids, our Ground Covers and Woodland Rock Plants. So when one plants the woodland pathway he can make it a veritable fairyland. Masses of Azalea, Rhododendrons and Laurel and shrubs like Leatherwood, Spicebush and the Viburnums and great numbers of ferns, large and small, may be used as a background or frame for the wondrous beauty of our woodland wildflowers.

Just at the entrance to the woodland pathway where the ground is moist and the sunlight plays for at least half the day would be a splendid place to plant the first of these, the

MEADOW ANEMONE (Anemone canadensis). Not many varieties of plants are easier to grow than this, and not many are more beautiful. Sometimes, if the ground is quite damp and rich, it grows two feet tall, but more often from twelve to fifteen inches. The flowers, one to two inches broad, are snowy white and blossom over a long period, mostly from May to July, but continuing until well into late summer, as a secondary crop of buds appears. Under favorable conditions, the plant spreads rapidly from the roots, and, although it grows wild over almost all of northern North America, it lends distinction to any cultivated garden or wild planting.

43

AMERICAN WOOD ANEMONE or WINDFLOWER (Anemone quinquefolia). In a somewhat similar location as regards sunlight, but somewhat drier, one might plant the little Windflower. I do not know how it got its name, but maybe because it is so fragile that it seems as if a strong wind might blow it away. The roots are threadlike and creeping, and in May the delicate white blossoms, about an inch broad, seem all out of proportion in size to the slender plant, which is four to seven inches tall.

RUE ANEMONE (Anemonella thalictroides) very closely resembles the Windflower in size and appearance, but the flowers are just a little smaller and are borne several to the stem. Be sure to plant these airy little wildflowers where they will not be crowded out by such strong growers as the Meadow Anemone.

CANADA WILDGINGER (Asarum canadense). Creeping erratically along the ground as if it is not sure just where it is going, the Wild-ginger hesitates every few inches to send up its large, downy, heart-shaped leaves, which are three to six inches broad, to a height of four or five inches. In April and May the reddish brown, bellshaped flowers, about an inch across, lie prostrate on the ground or sometimes buried in debris. The aromatic flavor of the root is responsible for the common name of the plant. From the southern Appalachians we get the Mottled Wildginger (Asarum shuttleworthi), which has mottled leaves.

COHOSH BUGBANE (Cimicifuga racemosa). Picturesque in the extreme are the pure white flowers of the Cohosh Bugbane, which grow in narrow racemes one to two feet long on top of a four to six foot stem. Rich black soil, where it is moist but not too wet, and with plenty of shade, is an ideal place to grow the Cohosh, which naturally is very common in the southern Appalachian region. The Cohosh blossoms in July and August. It may be increased by dividing the woody roots.

AMERICAN BUGBANE (Cimicifuga americana). Supremely artistic, the flowers of the American Bugbane grace the woodlands of late June. The panicled flower head, divided into laterals, which in turn are subdivided, makes this flower one of the most attractively arranged of any native plant. For combining in bouquets with other flowers no garden grown Astilbe can approach it. Where there is too much sun the flowers have a tendency to be cream colored, but in the shade or if brought into the house to open they are pure white. The plant attains a height of approximately two feet and may be increased by dividing.

CRINKLEROOT (Dentaria diphylla). The Crinkleroot is one of our earliest spring flowers and blossoms in company with Hepaticas, Springbeauty, Bloodroot, and Blue Cohosh. It likes rich, fairly moist soil and increases rapidly by means of creeping root stalks. The flowers, which are white, are borne in rather loose racemes on stems about a foot tall.

CUT TOOTHWORT or PEPPERROOT (Dentaria laciniata) closely resembles the Crinkleroot, except for its cutleaf foliage. It grows just a little taller. The Pepperroot enjoys the company of such plants as Wakerobin and Merrybells.

MISTFLOWER (Eupatorium coelistinum) is a plant from the Central States closely related to Joe-pye-weed and Boneset, but I always think of Joe Pye and Boneset with their big rough characters as being the boys of the family and the Mistflower and Snow Thoroughwort as the feminine members. The bright blue Ageratumlike blossoms of the Mistflower, which grows two feet tall in the open woods, depict grace and beauty, so lacking in their big brothers. It blossoms in August and September.

SNOW THOROUGHWORT (Eupatorium urticaefolium) is a splendid companion for the Mistflower, growing just a little taller, sometimes as high as three feet, and the broad flower heads in August and September are purest white. It is very easily grown in moist shade.

WILD FALSE FOXGLOVE (Gerardia virginica). Where the woodland pathway winds over dry, ledgy places one may find the Wild False Foxglove. In August the two foot spikes of purest yellow flowers, resembling the cultivated Foxglove in shape and size, give one of the clearest colors of the woods. It seems to have a peculiar affinity for oak trees, but is not too easily transplanted.

GOLDENSEAL (Hydrastis canadensis). Like the Ginseng, the Goldenseal has for a century been ceaselessly hunted for its thick yellow root stalk, which is used medicinally. The single, greenish white flower, borne at the top of a single broad leaf, is not showy. The value of the Goldenseal is in its romantic history rather than its actual beauty.

WATERLEAF (Hydrophyllus virginianum). In the rich, moist woods, the Virginia Waterleaf, which blossoms in midsummer, somewhat resembles the smaller growing Crinkleroot of early spring, but the flowers of the Waterleaf have a purplish tinge and the plant grows to two feet in height.

FALSE RUE ANEMONE (Isopyrum biternatum), from the thickets of the Central States, blossoms in May and gives an effect similar to the Windflower and Rue Anemone, with its finely cut foliage, white flowers and delicate bearing.

TWINLEAF (Jeffersonia diphylla). The Twinleaf is an early spring flowering plant from the Central States with pure white blossoms somewhat resembling Hepaticas. After blossoming, the plant attains an ultimate height of twelve to fifteen inches. It gets its name from the leaves, which are divided into two entire divisions. We find it a very easy and attractive wildflower to grow here in New England. It simply requires good soil and hardwoods shade such as is suited to the Sharplobe Hepatica or the Bloodroot. Twinleaf is propagated from seed or division.

CANADA MAYFLOWER (Maianthemum canadense). Growing generally throughout the woods of northern North America, the Wild Lily-of-the-valley or Canada Mayflower will almost form a ground cover in favorable locations. The lovely little racemes of pure white, fragrant, fluffy flowers rise to a height of about four inches the last of May, and are followed by a small cluster of red berries later in the season. The plant spreads either by creeping root stalks or by seed.

VIRGINIA BLUEBELLS (Mertensia virginica). Probably no plant native to North America is so widely and extensively used in wild gardens or even in formal planting as the Virginia Bluebells. From Central New York westward and southward Nature has planted it liberally, but here in New England we must do the planting ourselves.

The Virginia Bluebell grows easily in full sun but better in partial shade. The clusters of nodding, tubular blossoms open bright pink and turn to clear baby blue. Sometimes plants occur that retain their bright pink coloring throughout the blossoming season, and then again we occasionally find one that is pure white. It should be planted liberally for effect in the woods, and one should also consider that the tops die down in midsummer. From late July until the ground freezes is the ideal time for planting this beautiful wildflower.

It is propagated generally from seed, but if you wish to increase plants of a particular color it is necessary to divide the fleshy roots, which, as they grow old, naturally break up into smaller and newer sections.

THE PYROLAS. For some years we were unable to grow the Pyrolas successfully. Scientists told us that they were of parasitic nature, but after observing their habits we found that this does not seem to be the case. The plant increases in number by means of a slender creeping root stalk. After it has blossomed the basal leaves will remain green throughout the rest of that summer and the following spring and then die. In the meantime these creeping root stalks may travel as far as twelve or fifteen inches from the mother plant before forming a new bud, from which the plant of the next season will grow. It is useless to move the plant that has blossomed, but, in very early spring or autumn, great care should be taken to secure the new bud at the end of the creeping root stalk, which will form the plant for the following season. The fact that a plant moved in blossom or after going out of bloom will remain green throughout the fall and the next spring and then die is probably the reason that it has been regarded as of parasitic nature.

ROUNDLEAF PYROLA (Pyrola americana) grows wild in the somewhat poorer, lighter soils of the northern woods, frequently among Poplars or White Birches. The fragrant, waxy white, drooping, bellshaped flowers are borne in June and July on terminal racemes six to ten inches tall. The round basal leaves are evergreen.

SHINLEAF (Pyrola elliptica) is similar in growth and habits to the Roundleaf Pyrola except that the leaves are elliptical in shape, they do not lie so flat on the ground and are not evergreen.

ONE-FLOWERED PYROLA (Moneses uniflora). A beautiful little plant closely related to the Shinleafs, but found growing generally under pine trees, the Moneses bears in June a single beautiful waxy white flower on a four to six inch stem. It is very fragrant. Propagation is the same as for the Shinleafs. Do not be too sure of success in growing the One-flowered Pyrola, but if you can make it grow it is well worth every effort.

EARLY WOODBETONY (Pedicularis canadensis). One of the most curiously colored wildflowers is the Woodbetony, a native of the dry woods. The foliage is somewhat Tansy-like and the blossoms are borne on very short spikes at the top of five to six inch stems. They are yellow and brown in color, odd rather than showy. Woodbetony has the habit of dying down when transplanted and then the next season coming up as full of life as ever.

GREEK-VALERIAN (Polemonium reptans) grows from Central New York westward, and is generally catalogued by nurserymen as a rock plant. The Greek-valerian attains a height of a foot or more with equal breadth to the plant. The flowers closely resemble the flowers of the cultivated Jacobs Ladder and are borne over a long season from May until July. It is easily grown from seed or division and makes itself at home in the hardwoods or even in the full sun in the northern states.

FRINGED POLYGALA (Polygala paucifolia). Although having the habits of many of our ground covers and spreading from underground root stalks, the Fringed Polygala has so very few leaves that it makes a poor carpet. The showy, dark pink blossoms are borne on four to six inch stems in late May and early June and, from the appearance of the flowers, might easily be mistaken for a small Orchid, but of course they have nothing at all in common. Sometimes a pure white flowering plant is found and those of certain colors may be propagated by root cuttings. Like many Violets, the Fringed Polygala bears seed from unnoticed cleistogamous flowers. It grows in rather dry soil under hardwoods or to a considerable extent under evergreens throughout northeastern North America.

AMERICAN STARFLOWER (Trientalis americana). It is named from the starry shape of its pure white blossoms, and is one of the best of our tiny wildflowers of the woods in June. The single, fragile stems grow four to six inches tall from creeping root stalks. It is not advisable to transplant Starflower in blossom as it is necessary to plant the new bud which forms at the end of the slender root stalks in late summer and which may be several inches from the blossoming stem.

COMMON WOODSORREL (Oxalis acetosella). The dainty, pink-striped, solitary flowers one half to three fourths of an inch across and the three-parted leaves of the Woodsorrel typify fragility. The plant grows only three to four inches tall and flowers in June and July in moist woods. The Woodsorrel is probably the daintiest of all mid-summer woodland flowers. It spreads from creeping root stalks and seed.

VIOLET WOODSORREL (Oxalis violacea) grows in drier soil than the Common Woodsorrel and bears its blossoms several to the stalk during May and June.

FIREPINK (Silene virginica). Intense scarlet describes the coloring of the flowers of the Firepink. The plant grows only twelve to fifteen inches tall and is not an especially strong grower. In New England we find it does very well in open, rather dry soil, but in its own home, the southern Appalachians, is a native of the open woods. The Silenes are propagated from seed.

COMMON SPEEDWELL (Veronica officinalis) is an ordinary little cosmopolitan, creeping plant with bright blue flower spikes three to four inches tall and evergreen leaves. It is useful for growing under pine trees or almost any location in sun or shade, seeding freely, but not becoming a nuisance. This little plant, sometimes called Gipsy Weed, is taken as a matter of course.

CLAMBERING MONKSHOOD (Aconitum uncinatum) is a true Monkshood native to the southern Appalachian Mountains. The bright blue flowers are most noticeable in July. It likes to grow in strong, rich soil with neighboring bushes for its three to six foot stems to climb upon. It may be grown from divisions.

CLIMBING FUMITORY or MOUNTAIN FRINGE (Adlumia fungosa). After seeing the foliage of this dainty vine one would know right away that it belongs to the same family as the Dutchmans-breeches, but the Mountain Fringe is a true biennial and blossoms only one season. However, it seeds so freely that it may be depended upon to perpetuate itself in any moist thicket. The weak, slender stems climb ten to twenty feet over other bushes and small trees. The pale pink flowers in drooping racemes are borne from early summer until fall.

FRINGED BLEEDINGHEART (Dicentra eximia). For continuous bloom from spring until fall few flowers equal the Plumy Bleedingheart, a native of the Blue Ridge Mountains. It grows in moist shade and sometimes attains a height of eighteen inches. The spikes of flowers are pink when grown in shade, but fade badly in the sun. It is so easily grown that seed sown in midsummer will produce blossoming size plants by the next spring.

BLOODROOT
Sanguinaria canadensis

CHAPTER XIII

The Woodland Rock Garden

⫸⫸ ⫷⫷

WHEN Mother Nature sets out to make a rock garden she spends the first million years in a thorough preparation of the soil, pulverizing and disintegrating the limestone or slate ledges and cliffs, and hollowing out little pockets or seams where this material, mixed with the leafmold of untold centuries, may collect. Then, too, she provides for thorough drainage, and also for plenty of moisture from water trickling down the cliffs in springtime. And when, after numberless aeons have passed, she gets ready to plant this rock garden, she selects the choicest, loveliest flowers of the woods to put there.

Not many acid-loving plants are found in Nature's rock garden and the soil is most likely to be nearly neutral as regards acidity. Of course, human beings, always anxious to improve on Nature, may fill certain pockets with acid soil where a Moccasin Flower or Arbutus may grow, but why not plant these in their own natural location under the spreading pines and use the plants for the rock garden that Nature has provided?

Nature usually has her rock garden in partial shade. So why not follow her few simple rules— partial shade, trickling water in springtime, perfect drainage and pockets filled with pulverized stone and leafmold.

Besides the species which I am submitting to you as adapted to a woodland rock garden, there are many which I am describing elsewhere in this book. Particularly I would suggest the Baneberries, Clintonia, Moccasin Flower, Dalibarda, Iris cristata, Iris verna, Showy Orchis, Ginseng, Phlox in variety, Solomonseal, Blue Cohosh, Trilliums, Violets and many species of native ferns such as Maidenhair, Bladderfern, Ebony Spleenwort, Maidenhair Spleenwort, Rockfern, Oakfern and Christmas Fern.

51

DUTCHMANS-BREECHES (Dicentra cucullaria). Growing from Missouri and Kansas northward and eastward, the Dutchmans-breeches is very much at home on the shelving rocks where the plant food of centuries has accumulated. The feathery, fernlike foliage grows from a small white bulb not over an inch in diameter, that readily breaks up into many small sections, which may be planted to form new bulbs. Or it may spread from seed. The blossoms, on six inch stalks, resemble inverted trousers with a golden waistline and are borne several pairs to the stem. After blossoming in April, the leaves stay green until June, when they die down. The bulb, however, continues growing through the summer, and Nature depends upon the leaves of Herb Robert, Spleenworts and other small ferns and plants to furnish foliage for the rest of the season.

SQUIRRELCORN (Dicentra canadensis) is very similar to the Dutchmans-breeches in habit, except that the blossoms have a pink waistline and the plant grows from a small yellow bulb resembling a kernel of corn, which gives the plant its name.

BLOODROOT (Sanguinaria canadensis) is a native of the entire eastern half of the United States and known to everyone. It is one of our most easily grown wildflowers, and its pure white blossoms on stems six to eight inches tall in April are very beautiful. It will thrive under many varying conditions and is a good plant for the amateur. It is propagated readily from seed, which blossoms the second or third year after sowing, or from division of the root, preferably in autumn, giving from two to three new plants each year. The leaves of the Bloodroot are beautiful until late summer, when they die down.

AMERICAN COLUMBINE (Aquilegia canadensis) is a rock plant par excellence, and grows wild from Texas northward and eastward. It grows equally well in sun or shade, although the farther South it is grown the more shade it naturally prefers. The many-branched blossom stalks with the glorious flowers of red and yellow are used in New England with the long-stemmed Violet and Lilacs for decorating the soldiers' graves on Memorial Day. The American Columbine is easily grown from seed, which, if sown in May, will produce flowering size plants the following spring.

COLORADO COLUMBINE (Aquilegia caerulea) gives us wonderful large blossoms of blue and white, but the plant itself is very fragile and, in the East, shortlived. It is unfortunate that only a small percentage of the seed sold for Colorado Columbine is true to name. If it is not permitted to make seed the plant will become stronger and longer lived.

GOLDEN COLUMBINE (Aquilegia chrysantha), which comes to us from the mountains of northern Arizona, is well known to all gardeners. It is very vigorous and easy to grow, attaining a height of two to two and a half feet, and producing golden yellow flowers throughout the summer and fall. Probably it is too tall-growing for Nature's rock garden in the East, but I am mentioning it in connection with the other Columbines at this time.

HAREBELL or BLUEBELLS OF SCOTLAND (Campanula rotundifolia) is a native of nearly all the temperate world. It may be found growing in the open, sandy plains of Ontario or from a fissure in the rocks in rather dense shade on the banks of a small New England river. The seemingly fragile Bluebells of Scotland is one of the most persistent and courageous plants in existence. It may grow in the seams of a granite boulder in midriver, where it is crushed and pounded by the rushing high waters of spring and scalded by the torrid sun of midsummer, but, nevertheless, persist in producing its delicate blue bells from early June until the end of the autumn.

VIRGINIA SPRINGBEAUTY (Claytonia virginica). The dainty, pink-striped flowers of the Springbeauty blossom in early spring, growing from irregularly shaped bulbs, which Nature plants two to three inches below the surface. Although a native of the woods, it grows satisfactorily in open gardens, responds readily to culture, and increases rapidly.

PALE CORYDALIS (Corydalis glauca) is a beautiful biennial, which seeds itself freely, thus insuring its perpetuation. Although it may grow a little better in full sun, yet it is very satisfactory to grow among the ledges in partial shade. The branching flower stalks grow to two feet in height and the pink and yellow flowers are borne profusely over a considerable period in early summer. It is a native of northern United States and Canada.

THE WHITE TROUTLILY (Erythronium albidum) is the freest bloomer of all the Troutlilies, and I find it the easiest to grow. It comes from the Central States, but makes itself at home in New England, producing seed and also spreading rapidly from underground root stalks, which produce new bulbs at their terminals. It is pure white with an occasional trace of purple.

COMMON TROUTLILY (Erythronium americanum) is plentiful over the entire eastern United States and Canada and is quite commonly called Adders-tongue or Dogtooth Violet. The leaves are much more beautiful than those of the White Troutlily, which is well, because it mats its bulbs so thickly that they have scarcely room to develop and it blossoms much less freely than its white relative from the Central States.

CALIFORNIA TROUTLILY (Erythronium californicum). The Pacific coast sends us several kinds of Troutlily which do well in rich, moist shade in New England. The California Troutlily is a fine little species, bearing several clear yellow flowers to a stalk and is apparently the easiest to grow of the western ones.

HENDERSON TROUTLILY (Erythronium hendersoni) produces a smaller flower, which is a rich royal purple, and is not so vigorous a grower.

LEMON TROUTLILY (Erythronium citrinum) closely resembles our eastern yellow Troutlily, but is a clearer yellow in color and with less mottled leaves.

HERB ROBERT (Geranium robertianum) is not happy unless growing on the rocky ledges, where it attains a height of about twelve inches. The reddish stems are branching and the small rose-colored blossoms are borne more or less all summer. The leaves are evergreen, dying in the spring.

WILD GERANIUM (Geranium maculatum) grows to a height of about a foot with flowers much larger than those of the Herb Robert, but of a more purplish pink. Both the Wild Geraniums grow extensively over eastern North America and are readily transplanted.

COMMON BISHOPSCAP or MITREWORT (Mitella diphylla) is found growing equally well in the clefts of the ledges or on hummocks in the bogs. The Mitrewort, or Bishopscap, gets its name from the shape of the flowers, which are white and grow on slender spikes a foot tall during May. It is grown from its black, shiny seeds.

FOAMFLOWER (Tiarella cordifolia). Here is a plant, which, while not strictly a rock plant, as it grows equally well on the forest floor, may be utilized in connection with naturalistic planting among the rocks.

Perhaps it is more at home among the rock heaps than it is in the rock garden, for we find it growing beautifully in the tumbled masses of jagged boulders at the foot of the shaded cliffs. It is well to remember that it prefers acid soil. The fluffy white flower heads rise to a height of six to eight inches in May. The leaves remain green all winter and the plant is propagated by means of its runners in the same manner as strawberries reproduce.

SHARPLOBE Hepatica (Hepatica acutiloba) is a natural rock plant, growing vigorously in neutral soil. The foliage is evergreen and the blossoms vary from white to pink, blue and purple, and occasionally one will be found that is almost red. The Sharplobe Hepatica is well known throughout eastern North America and is one of our finest plants. It is propagated by dividing the plants and by this means plants of certain colors may be increased.

ROUNDLOBE HEPATICA (Hepatica triloba) differs from the Sharplobe Hepatica not only in the shape of its leaves, but it usually declines to grow in the same vicinity and chooses as its companions the Moccasin Flower, Fringed Polygala, Lowbush Blueberry and other plants requiring intensely acid soil. The Roundlobe Hepatica, while varying in color from white to dark blue with occasional pinks, is more likely to be pale blue. The plant is not so strong a grower as its mountain relative, but both respond readily to cultivation. Just remember that the Roundlobe Hepatica must have acid soil and the Sharplobe Hepatica the neutral or slightly alkaline soil and you will get along nicely with both.

CRESTED IRIS (Iris cristata) is without doubt one of the finest little rock plants. Although growing only four to six inches in height, this little chap struts along the rocks as gayly as if he were the biggest of his family, and in early May the flowers make a sky blue carpet. Sometimes snow white flowers (Iris cristata alba) are found. Of course all Iris increases rapidly by dividing the clumps at any time during the year, although midsummer is perhaps the best time if they are not permitted to dry out before becoming reestablished.

VERNAL IRIS (Iris verna) is the tiniest of our native Iris, growing only about four inches tall, even smaller than Iris cristata, with pale blue flowers in May. It grows naturally among such plants as Rhododendrons, Azaleas and Galax, therefore requires a very acid soil in which to do its best, also rather dense shade.

VIRGINIA SAXIFRAGE (Saxifraga virginiensis) grows where the shade is not too dense and is found even more commonly in full sun, particularly at a higher altitude. It seeds itself freely and the white flowers are generally borne in artistic clusters in earliest spring.

CHAPTER XIV

Color on the Hillside

-»»-»» «-«

IN midsummer, when the colorful flowers of springtime have gone, and the full growth of foliage has rendered the shade of the woodlands so dense that few plants are in bloom there, then we have to look to the open hillsides to find the bright colors, which, after all, appeal to our highly cultured and self-satisfied people of today as much as they ever did to our primitive forbears. Many of the plants which grow in the open sun and blossom during the hot, dry weather of midsummer are deep-rooting in order to secure the moisture which they require for their development. Most of them are very easily propagated from seed, but the Butterflyweed is readily grown from root cuttings and the Fireweeds spread from creeping root stalks.

The wildflowers which we are including in this group do not by any means comprise all that grow successfully on the open hillsides, but are selected as examples of plants that may be used in developing midsummer color in a rather difficult location.

BUTTERFLYWEED (Asclepias tuberosa). "Gorgeous" describes the coloring of this member of the Milkweed family, for the flaming orange or reddish blossoms justify the use of this word in describing them. The plant itself is a native of southern New England, New York State and south and westward. It grows to a height of one to two feet and is readily grown from seed sown in spring or early summer, which develops plants large enough to blossom the following year. It is also easily propagated by root cuttings and this means may be used to increase the number of plants of a certain color. It requires plenty of room and sunshine to develop to its best. The Butterflyweed is a very long-lived perennial.

THE BAPTISIAS are dry land and leguminous plants, which draw their nitrogen from the air, not only for immediate use, but store it up in little nodules on the roots for future needs. They are very substantial

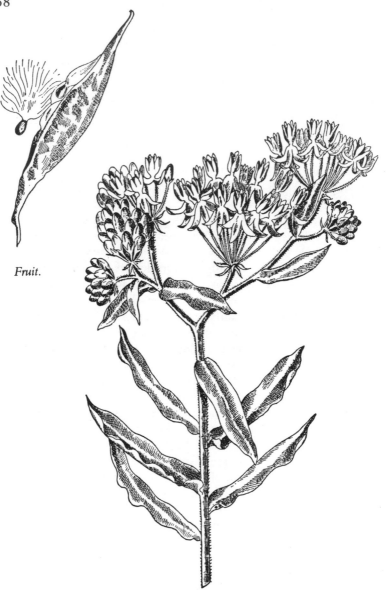

Fruit.

BUTTERFLYWEED
Asclepias tuberosa

and when established seldom need to be renewed. The species here described are natives of Southern and Central United States.

They require plenty of room for development and should be planted singly or in small groups for best results.

WHITE WILD-INDIGO (Baptisia leucantha) attains a height of three feet and blossoms in erect spikes of pure white, pea-shaped flowers in June and July.

CREAM WILD-INDIGO (Baptisia bractcata) is the earliest one, but instead of being erect the spikes are drooping and the flowers are creamy white. It grows only twelve to eighteen inches tall.

YELLOW WILD-INDIGO (Baptisia tinctoria) is the latest to bloom. It grows two to three feet high, and the flowers are bright yellow on semi-drooping, branching spikes.

BLUE WILD-INDIGO (Baptisia australis). A leguminous plant from thc South, yet Blue Wild-Indigo readily adapts itself to almost any location that is not too wet. It makes a large clump two to three feet tall and about as broad. The spikes of blue flowers are borne erect in June.

LOW POPPY-MALLOW (Callirhoe involucrata) is a sprawling, trailing vine very prevalent on our western plains, and its single, saucer-shaped flowers, two inches across, are probably the nearest to true magenta in color of any flower we have. They are not the shade so often described as "rosy-purple," but a clear, brilliant, delightful color, which cannot be described by mere man. The fullgrown plants spread over three feet and they blossom over a long season in midsummer.

Callirhoe triangulata is an erect-growing Poppy-mallow from the prairies. It attains a height of eighteen inches. The blossoms are not so clear a color as the foregoing variety, and the root is thick and fleshy like a parsnip. It should be mulched to prevent heaving by frost in the spring.

BLOOMING SALLY or FIREWEED (Epilobium angustifolium). Fireweeds are so called because of their prevalence on burned-over hill-sides, and they might well be called Fireweeds because the masses of bloom in mid-summer, by a sufficient stretching of the imagination, might be considered to look like a well-behaved bonfire.   For the benefit of the few who may not be acquainted with this plant, I will say that it is a rather tall-growing (three to four feet), but not awkward, plant, covered in midsummer with spires of rosy-purple flowers, but as it usually blossoms in company with yellow flowers their colors do not clash. The plant spreads rapidly from seed and also from creeping root stalks.

There is a larger growing pure white variety of Fireweed, Epilobium angustifolium alba, found growing on Camel's Hump Mountain in Vermont by Mr. James E. Mitchell. This variety is a decided addition to the list of wildflowers for midsummer blooming, and when better known will probably be extensively used in naturalizing.

COMMON POKEBERRY (Phytolacca americana). Here is another tall-growing wild plant with a parsnip-like root. It has rather conspicuous stems, which, when they reach a height of about three feet, produce racemes of white flowers in midsummer. It is perhaps most conspicuous in early autumn for its dark red or purplish berries, which are borne profusely. It is called Garget Plant by the farmers of New England because of its use as a remedy for this disease among cattle. It also furnishes young America with a glorious supply of purple juice for making war paint and writing black hand letters.

CAROLINA ALLSPICE (Thermopsis caroliniana). The Southern States sent us this very vigorous and attractive wildflower. It is a legume, growing three feet in height and bearing many spikes of pea-shaped, yellow flowers to the plant. Thermopsis is a really fine plant, not only for naturalizing on the hot hillsides and on the sandy lands where so many wildflowers fail, but it is also a wonderfully good perennial for the background of the hardy border.

BLACK-EYED-SYSAN (Rudbeckia hirta) is well known of course to everyone. My own young daughter at the age of six advised me quite appropriately that she had found some "chocolate daisies," for they certainly look very much like oldtime twenty cent chocolates surrounded by rays of yellow petals.

A great many people have tried to transplant the Black-eyed-susans and have met with disappointment. This does not mean that it is hard to transplant, because it is not, but the eastern species, Rudbeckia hirta, is a biennial. However, the Central West furnishes us with a true perennial species, Rudbeckia newmanni, but the "chocolates" are a little more elongated than those of the eastern kind.

SUN-DIAL LUPINE (Lupinus perennis). This is the native eastern

Blue Lupine, found growing usually in dry, sandy soil. It is so very well known that description is unnecessary. Sometimes white or pink flowers are also found in the wild. Whenever a substantial plant is needed for rather sandy soil the Wild Lupine is desirable. Being a leguminous plant it draws nitrogen from the air for its own use and also to store up in the nodules on its roots, thus enriching the soil wherever it grows, but of course it should not be planted near fragile plants, for, seeding itself quite freely, it will overrun them.

WINELEAF CINQUEFOIL (Potentilla tridentata). My first plants of this low, shrubby perennial were obtained on the Maine coast, where they grow in sandy, gravelly soil or on the dry, exposed cliffs. The starry white flowers are borne on slender three inch stems rising from almost prostrate tufts of glossy, dark green foliage in early summer.

In autumn the leaves of this Cinquefoil become wine color, which gives it its name and is the reason the plant is so desirable for exposed, sunny locations.

BLUETS (Houstonia caerulea) is also called Quaker Ladies, Innocence and Eyebright, although if this last name were changed to Bright Eyes it would seem better. With the common field Violet, the Wild Strawberry and the Early Everlasting they carpet the hillside pastures in early spring. The Bluets radiate cheerfulness and friendliness.

If a locality suits them they populate it by the millions. If it does not they do not grow at all. Eastern New England is particularly favored and from early May until into June acres may be covered with the tiny light blue flowers, which grow on two to four inch stems.

It is sometimes considered a biennial because the mother plant dies after blossoming, but before she dies she arranges a family right around her by means of creeping root stalks, which perpetuates the plant. One often finds Bluets flowering in late fall. The plants are grown from seed or by dividing the clumps. When not in blossom they form neat little green tufts about an inch across and half an inch tall.

PEATPINK (Silene pennsylvanica) is a rather uncommon and much sought for little plant, which grows in loose, gravelly soil or on the open cliffs of the Atlantic coast states. The dense tufts of foliage with their bright pink single flowers an inch broad grow from thick surface root stalks to a height of four to six inches. It is undoubtedly one of our best and most unobtainable wildflowers for a sunny rock planting.

AZURE SALVIA (Salvia azurea). From the Rocky Mountains the

62

BLUETS
Hedyotis caerulea
(formerly *Houstonia caerulea*)

Blue Sage has gone forth to find its place in gardens the world over. It grows to a height of two to three feet. The branching flower spikes produce the sky blue blossoms over a period of several weeks in late summer. When once established, Azure Salvia is very permanent and not at all inclined to be weedy. It prefers dry, sunny soil.

GOLDEYE-GRASS (Hypoxis hirsuta). If any plant is indifferent as to its location it is the tiny Goldeye-grass, or Yellow Stargrass, listed by botanists as growing in dry, sandy soil, yet found commonly growing in bogs in company with the Calopogon. I am grouping it with the hillside plants because it associates so nicely with the Blue-eyed-grass. Beginning to flower in late spring, it continues throughout most of June and July, growing not quite so tall as its blue-eyed companion, but yielding its tiny yellow flowers in umbels opening one at a time.

The Yellow Stargrass as it is often called grows from a small bulb or corm and when it first comes up in the springtime may very easily be mistaken for grass and weeded out.

BLUE-EYED-GRASS (Sisyrinchium angustifolium). From northeastern United States and Canada west to the Rocky Mountains the tiny Blue-eyed-grass is found. It belongs to the Iris family, but it is so small as to be mistaken for grass unless it is in bloom. This little plant with its prettily tufted habit of growth delights in sunny fields and hillsides where the sod is not too heavy nor the soil too wet. From May into July it produces starry blue flowers on six to twelve inch stems.

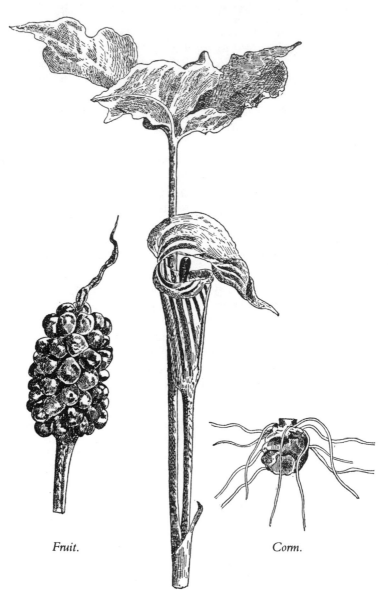

Fruit.

Corm.

JACK-IN-THE-PULPIT
Arisaema triphyllum

CHAPTER XV

Some Plants With Bright Berries

-»»- -»»- -««- -««-

L ATE summer would be a drab season in the forest were it not for the brilliant fruit of many kinds of shrubs and wildflowers, for the shade is then so dense that very few plants can bloom in the woods at this season. But Nature has given us many kinds of spring-blooming wildflowers that have brilliant fruit in late summer, and the monotony of the forest may be broken by flashes of scarlet, white or blue.

Besides the plants mentioned in this chapter, others which produce attractively colored fruit, and which are considered elsewhere in this book, are the Sarsaparillas, Creeping Snowberry, Bitter Nightshade, Canada Mayflower, Cucumber-root, Partridgeberry, Pokeberry, Mayapple, Trilliums and the Checkerberry.

ROSY TWISTEDSTALK (Streptopus roseus) is the first of the wildflowers to ripen its conspicuously brilliant fruit, and in late July the roadsides and upland hardwoods are enlivened by its brilliant show of color. The light scarlet fruits, one-third of an inch in diameter, are borne all along under the three-parted stems of the plant, which grows to two feet in height. They look like little tomatoes. In May the rose colored flowers are borne one or two from the axil of each of the upper leaves and would be attractive were they not concealed so much by the foliage.

TWISTEDSTALK (Streptopus amplexifolium) grows to a height of three feet with more glaucous foliage than its smaller relative and with larger, more elongated fruit, which ripens two weeks later. The flowers are greenish white in color , but it is the fruit of both the Twistedstalks that renders them so valuable to the wildflower gardener. They are propagated from seed. Peter Rabbit has a decided liking for the Twistedstalks and unless they are guarded he will keep the plants well trimmed. Birds are very fond of the fruit.

65

JACK-IN-THE-PULPIT (Arisaema triphyllum). Jack likes children and children like him. They like him so well that they quite often pull him up from his home in the moist woods and transplant him somewhere else. If it is not too hot and dry he usually grows good-naturedly. Sometimes he has a green pulpit, sometimes a striped green and brown one. Jack produces a cluster of brilliant red berries, which fall to the ground in early September and germinate so readily that the following year he may likely be surrounded by a numerous colony of little preachers. Sometimes I wonder just what he preaches about. Perhaps he is just telling the boys and girls not to taste the bulb from which he grows, for if one does this it surely takes a long time to get the face straightened out again.

DRAGONROOT or GREEN DRAGON (Arisaema dracontium) grows in the Central States. It is really not so savage as it sounds, but is a very peculiar form in which the spadix is long and tapering like a bayonet. The Green Dragon blossoms later than Jack-in-the-pulpit and does not grow quite so tall.

BLUE COHOSH (Caulophyllum thalictroides). The young shoots of the Blue Cohosh, unfolding in early spring, are exceptionally beautiful in their robes of royal purple. When the plant reaches its full height of eighteen to twenty-four inches in late April and May it blossoms, but the yellow flowers with purple sepals are not very conspicuous. However, in August the Blue Cohosh again offers brilliant color in the form of its glaucous blue berries. It is easily grown from seed.

BUNCHBERRY (Cornus canadensis) grows naturally clear across northern North America and into eastern Asia. This plant is a boon companion of Bluebeads (Clintonia borealis). It spreads from creeping root stalks and forms a carpet on the ground in the moist woods where there is sufficient acid in the soil.

The flowers of the Bunchberry are pure white, four-petaled, and produced so freely as to form a sheet of white on the forest floor. The fruit ripens in late summer, is scarlet in color and borne in bunches, which gives the plant its name. The berries, while edible, are quite tasteless, and one really does not enjoy them unless very hungry. Bunchberry is usually transplanted in small sods and is not difficult to grow in moist, acid shade.

BLUEBEADS (Clintonia borealis). Very common in the mountains of eastern North America and usually found in company with the

Bunchberry, the Clintonia belongs to the Lily-of-the-valley family and the leaves resemble the leaves of that plant. In May the flower stem rises to a height of about a foot and produces several greenish yellow, lilylike blossoms, but in August the clusters of shining dark blue fruit are one of the conspicuous features of the woods.

Many people think the Clintonia is hard to transplant, whereas this is not so. In late summer the plant sends out two or three underground runners several inches in length and at the end of each runner is produced a bud, which forms a new plant for the following year. The mother plant, having fulfilled her mission, does not grow the next spring, and those who failed with the Clintonia have usually transplanted only the mother without the new buds, consequently they have no plant the following season. The Clintonia insists on acid soil conditions with plenty of leafmold to conserve the moisture.

QUEENCUP (Clintonia uniflora) was sent to me by a wildflower lover from Alaska, but it also grows wild in the mountains of Oregon and Washington. The leaves of the Clintonias are all similar, but the Queencup, which is doing well under our New England conditions, produces a single, upright, fragrant flower of pure white.

SPECKLED CLINTONIA (Clintonia umbellulata) came to us accidentally in a clump of Shortia from the southern mountains. It bears several small, erect, white flowers and has black berries. Compared with the other Clintonias it is not so attractive.

SMALL SOLOMONSEAL (Polygonatum biflorum). Common in the woods of eastern North America, the Solomonseal is not particularly beautiful for its flowers, which are green bells usually hanging in pairs from the underside of the arching, two foot stalks in late May and June, but it is attractive for the steely blue fruits, which follow these blossoms in late summer. The Solomonseal gets its name from the peculiar scars on the zigzag root stalks, each scar representing a year's growth of the root and the place where the stalk of the previous year was borne.

Under cultivation the blossoms and fruit are often borne in bunches of three or four instead of pairs.

GREAT SOLOMONSEAL (Polygonatum commutatum) is a veritable giant, growing to a height of four feet and bearing its yellowish green blossoms in late June. It prefers the lowland thickets or even open meadows along the streams, while its smaller relative makes his home in the uplands. The Great Solomonseal grows northward only to southern New England, but is perfectly hardy if planted above this range. The Solomonseals appreciate good care and rich soil and respond wonderfully well to a little cultivation or stirring of the soil around them during the summer.

FALSE SOLOMONSEAL (Smilacina racemosa) is a roadside plant growing generally over temperate North America. It bears its fluffy white racemes of flowers on two foot stalks in late May and early June, and later in the summer produces a crop of glassy, red berries. It is one of the most easily grown wildflowers in sun or partial shade.

STARRY FALSE SOLOMONSEAL (Smilacina stellata) has a smaller cluster of flowers, and the berries are green with black stripes, or else entirely black.

RED BANEBERRY (Actaea rubra). Perhaps the most desirable of all plants with bright colored berries are the Baneberries. The Red Baneberry grows to two feet in height, with very attractive, fluffy, white flower heads in early May. In late July it produces fruit of intense scarlet turning to crimson. It likes the rich, moist soil of the roadside or edge of the forest. It is propagated from seed, which must be sown in the autumn or else stratified, and usually requires two years for germination. Seedlings begin to blossom at the age of three years, but the plant increases in size and beauty for several years more. It is very long lived and when once established is one of the most permanent wildflowers.

WHITE BANEBERRY (Actaea alba) grows taller than the Red Baneberry. The flowers in spring are practically identical, but the White Baneberry grows deeper in the woods than the Red, preferring more shade, or perhaps it does not care for human company so much. The fruit of the White Baneberry, glistening white with a black speck on the end like dolls' eyes, ripens nearly three weeks later than the Red Baneberry. Except for its desire to live deeper in the woods, the habits of the White Baneberry are the same as those of the Red.

AMERICAN GINSENG (Panax quinquefolium). This is the Ginseng of commerce, that has been hunted incessantly since colonial days and is probably just about as plentiful now as it ever was, thus showing just how hard it is to really exterminate a plant species. The Ginseng grows slowly and is a very long lived plant. When fully grown it reaches a height of eighteen inches. The greenish white flowers are not conspicuous, but the bright red fruit, borne in an upright cluster from the axis of the three compound leaves and ripening in early September, is very much so. Ginseng is invariably grown from seed, but it requires several years to bring a plant to blossoming size. It has a peculiar affinity for Butternut and Basswood trees and is scarcely ever found wild except in their proximity.

CHAPTER XVI

Our Native Phlox

-»»-»»-«-«-

THERE is considerable variation in the habits of the many kinds of Phlox native to eastern North America, but they have one characteristic in common—all grow in rather dry soil. This family is one of the most useful, as they serve a wide range of purposes, from providing billowing waves of color in the woodland to low-growing splashes of blue or pink in a tiny rock garden. Phlox is easy to propagate, growing readily from seed, division or from cuttings. Always plant it where there is good drainage.

AMOENA or LOVELY PHLOX (Phlox amoena), from the southern Appalachians, is one of the easiest of Phlox species to grow, either in the sun or in open woodlands. It attains a height of four to six inches and blossoms about a week after the Phlox subulata, in May. At a little distance a mass of this Phlox appears to be bright pink, but close examination shows a trace of purple and if the blooms are brought into the house they will in a short time turn to an unattractive purplish shade. This Phlox is useful for rock gardens, borders or naturalizing.

BLUE PHLOX (Phlox divaricata), which grows from Central New York westward and southward is probably the most useful member of the wild Phlox family. It is used extensively for woodland planting, although it will grow in almost any location, attaining a height of twelve to fifteen inches. The color is blue with a trace of purple. A selected, clear blue strain is sold by nurserymen as Phlox divaricata laphami, and one also finds pure white blossoms of this variety. The Blue Phlox blossoms in May.

DOWNY PHLOX (Phlox pilosa), which grows thriftily in the open sunshine, is a contribution from the Middlewest. The lovely pink blossoms in June grow on stalks about a foot tall. It is easily grown and may be increased rapidly by division.

CREEPING PHLOX (Phlox reptans), which should be more generally used to provide patches of pink in the dry hardwoods shade, is another Phlox from the southern mountains. Phlox reptans actually prefers poor, thin, acid soil at which most wildflowers would tilt their noses in disgust. The blossom stalks are only four or five inches tall and the season of blooming is late May and early June. A creeping species, rooting as it travels.

CLEFT PHLOX (Phlox bifida). I think this is one of the best, although the least known. It came to us from the sandy lands of the Central West and the masses of clear blue flowers, whose petals radiate like the spokes of a wheel and broaden at the ends to form the rim, are peculiarly attractive during the last of May. It grows only three or four inches tall.

SMOOTH PHLOX (Phlox glaberrima) is the tallest member of the family, and also a native of the Middle West. The grasslike foliage attains a height of from two to three feet and produces pink flowers in midsummer. Glaberrima might well be used for naturalizing in waste corners in full sun.

MOUNTAIN PHLOX (Phlox ovata) is certainly one of the finest of wildflowers and more closely resembles the cultivated Phlox, Phlox decussata, than any of the other American species. It comes from the South and is decidedly useful in open hardwoods shade or in full sun. It grows about twelve to fifteen inches tall and the large flowers, blossoming in June, are clear rose pink.

MOSS PHLOX (Phlox subulata). This immigrant has so thoroughly naturalized itself in eastern United States that it should be mentioned. Growing in the poorest of soils, it has taken almost complete possession of any number of our semi-neglected old cemeteries, making them colorful indeed at Memorial Day or a little earlier. Wide variations in color are found, and named varieties of pure white and shades of blue and pink are sold by the trade. Phlox subulata must have full sun.

WILD SWEET WILLIAM (Phlox maculata) is native from northern Pennsylvania southward, and the pink or purple, and sometimes white, flowers are borne in compact clusters. The plant attains a height of one to two feet.

WOOD LILY
Lilium philadelphicum

CHAPTER XVII

Wild Lilies

⟫⟫⟫ ⟪⟪⟪

SOME kind of wild Lily seems to grow in nearly every section of the United States. They may be depended on to add stateliness and grace to the wildflower garden as well as to the formal border.

Propagation of Lilies may be by seed, which germinates anywhere from two weeks to two years after being planted, by offshoots from the mother bulb, or from scales. Plant the seed of our native species in moist, but well drained soil, preferably under artificial shade, and the resulting bulbs will usually blossom the third year after it is sown. Lilies should not be planted alone, but among other plants, particularly ferns, which will keep the ground moist and cool so that the heat of the sun's rays cannot injure the bulb. Although native Lilies grow both in sun and shade, yet practically all species seem to grow a little closer to perfection in partial shade.

Lilies are a favorite food with rabbits and it is very exasperating to find that Peter has stripped a bed of all its seed pods in a single night.

CANADA or MEADOW LILY (Lilium canadense) is very common in moist meadows and roadside thickets from New England westward and southward to the plains. In moist shade it sometimes attains a height of five feet, and its drooping flowers, borne several to the stem, vary in color from pale yellow to almost red. The bulbs are planted by Nature about six inches below the surface of the ground. It blossoms in early July.

ORANGECUP or WOOD LILY (Lilium philadelphicum) is one of the plants which absolutely insist on acid soil, growing naturally in the dry pine barrens and blueberry fields of northeastern United States. Its companions are quite likely to be Trailing Arbutus and Pink Moccasin Flower, as well as the Lowbush Blueberry. The upright flowers are borne on stems one to two feet tall and are nearly red in color. It is a midsummer variety.

73

AMERICAN TURKSCAP LILY (Lilium superbum) is found from southern New England westward to Minnesota and southward. It is one of the most easily grown and one of the tallest native Lilies, reaching a height of five feet, and bearing its orange colored blossoms in profusion. It does not seem to be particular in its soil requirements, growing either in open, sandy soil or in the rich, black earth of the thickets. It blossoms later than the Meadow Lily.

CAROLINA LILY (Lilium carolinianum) is so nearly like the Turkscap Lily that one can hardly tell where one begins and the other leaves off, but it seems to me that the green markings in the flowers of the Carolina Lily are more broad than in the Turkscap and the blossom stalk does not grow quite so tall, nor produce flowers so freely.

GRAY'S LILY (Lilium grayi) is a small, dark red Lily from the South, which grows very nicely in the North, apparently preferring acid soil. It seldom exceeds three feet in height and bears many drooping flowers to the stem in late June. For open fields or thickets.

LEOPARD LILY (Lilium pardalinum). After failing two or three times with this Lily we finally planted it in rich, moist soil under artificial shade and it immediately became the most vigorous and prolific of all, reproducing very easily from scales and offshoots. In fact, a single bulb has produced several flowering bulbs for us in one year's time. It grows about two feet tall with heavier foliage than our eastern Lilies, and the large, orange-spotted flowers blossom much later in the summer.

LEMON LILY (Lilium parryi) is a fragrant, clear yellow Lily from the Pacific coast, growing two to three feet tall. It should succeed under the same conditions as the Leopard Lily.

Very likely many other western Lilies would succeed under these conditions, but as we have not proven this yet I think it best not to prophesy success at this time.

CHAPTER XVIII

Flowers of the Fields

-->>> ->>> <<<- <<<-

THE open fields or meadows produce wildflowers in the most voluminous quantities. Regretfully I must admit that not all these are as desirable for planting in a wild garden or worthy of such solicitous care as most of our woodland flowers. Not that they are not beautiful or showy and produce immense splashes of color on a midsummer landscape, but some of them are ungrateful and bear out the saying that "Give a knave an inch and he will take an ell."

Happily, we are not obliged to place the blame for this ingratitude upon our native North American wildflowers to any extent, but on the European immigrants which have found lodging in this country through being brought in in grass seed.

If you are fortunate enough not to have them in your vicinity, by all means avoid planting the Devil's Paintbursh or Orange Hawkweed (Hieracium aurantiacum) and Viper's Bugloss or Blue Thistle (Echium vulgare). Nor is the Bladder Campion (Silene latifolia) particularly to be desired. All three of these plants have the habit of spreading rapidly from creeping root stalks as well as from seed and are likely to soon take possession of any field where they are given an opportunity. Some might include the White or Oxeye Daisy (Chrysanthemum leucanthemum), which is also an immigrant, in the list of undesirables, but I find it hard to maintain the antipathy for it that I have for the three foregoing robbers.

Originally, the meadows of New England were very free from flowering plants and weeds, probably because they were carved out of the forest. Not only immigrants from across the sea but adventurers from our own prairie states have come in to help brighten up the summer season in our eastern hayfields, but the western Americans have little tendency toward becoming nuisances.

75

The wildflowers which we shall consider in this chapter are those which I do not regard as serious pests. Of course our Meadow Lilies, Great Solomonseal, Meadow Anemone, the Fleabanes, Black-eyed-susans and New England Asters should be considered in making a meadow or open field planting, but they are described elsewhere.

PRAIRIE MEADOWSWEET (Filipendula rubra) is the wild Pink Spiraea of the Central West, cultivated extensively in gardens, but very easily naturalized in a moist, sunny location. It reaches a height of two to three feet, blossoms in July and is easily propagated from spreading root stalks.

CATTAIL GAYFEATHER (Liatris pycnostachya) is a splendid wildflower from the prairie states. It is the tallest of its family, reaching a height of three feet or more, and may also be distinguished from its very close relative, the Spike Gayfeather, in that it blossoms a week to ten days earlier. In August the long stalks of the Gayfeathers thickly set with thistlelike pinkish-lavender blossoms blend their color appropriately with the yellow flowers which prevail at this season of the year.

SPIKE GAYFEATHER (Liatris spicata) is the most commonly cultivated of all and is quite similar to the Cattail Gayfeather, except for being a little bit later and with finer foliage. The Gayfeathers are all crazy, for they start at the top of the spike and blossom downward over a long period, whereas nearly all flowers start to bloom at the bottom of the spike.

BUTTON GAYFEATHER (Liatris scariosa) does not grow so tall as the other species, but has larger individual flowers. A great many think it the most attractive of all, but of course that is a matter of opinion. The stalks grow about two feet tall and produce their attractive, thistlelike, lavender-pink flowers in September. The Gayfeathers are one of the easiest families to grow in open soil that has a tendency to be dry and sandy. All are propagated from seed or from division of old clumps.

THE PUCCOON (Lithospermum canescens) is from the open, sandy land of the Middle States and its clusters of golden yellow flowers on six to eighteen inch stems are produced in May and June. It is propagated from seed.

LANCE COREOPSIS (Coreopsis lanceolata). There is hardly a gardener but what is well acquainted with the perennial Coreopsis of the garden, but so many do not know that this is a native of Central United States. This, however, is the case, and it is easily naturalized in almost any location which is not extremely wet or extremely dry. Due to its habit of yielding its golden yellow blossoms from early summer until autumn it is very widely planted in gardens and this same reason recommends it for roadside or meadow planting.

EASTERN PENSTEMON (Penstemon hirsutus). In the dry, open woods of New England westward and southward the Eastern Penstemon grows one to two feet tall, producing lovely lavender-pink, tubular flowers from May to July. I find it grows successfully in full sun in Vermont, but the colors are not so bright as in partial shade. Penstemons are propagated either from seed or division of the Phloxlike plants.

FOXGLOVE PENSTEMON (Penstemon digitalis) is a white species growing about two feet tall and blossoming in midsummer.

TORREY PENSTEMON (Penstemon barbatus) is a showy crimson species from the Rocky Mountains most generally found under cultivation. It might well be called Firecracker Plant because the individual flowers on two foot stems resemble firecrackers in shape and color and are always in bloom by July fourth. Our western mountains will some day send many lovely species of Penstemons to the gardens of the world, but at present they are not grown much except by connoisseurs and experimenters.

VIRGINIA SPIDERWORT (Tradescantia virginiana). Although often described as a native of woods and thickets, I have seen the Spiderwort in greatest abundance in the Central West along railroad embankments in full sun and in the North I am quite certain it prefers open land. The Spiderwort varies greatly in color from pure white with blue centers, through varying shades of blue and violet, and pink forms are sometimes found also. It blossoms over an unusually long season from May until July, but to enjoy the flowers one must get up in the morning, as the petals usually fall in the middle of the day. Spiderwort is so easily grown and so well-behaved that it might be used extensively for naturalizing along stone walls or any waste places.

ZIGZAG SPIDERWORT (Tradescantia pilosa) is a smaller species with less conspicuous flowers also found in the North Central West, and this same section of the country also sends us a pink species, Tradescantia bracteata or BRACTED SPIDERWORT, but for all practical purposes Tradescantia virginiana is by far the best.

CULVERS-ROOT (Veronica virginica). I first got acquainted with this in Wisconsin where it was making itself at home and attractive along the fences and roadsides, but I have since learned that it grows wild from New England to Texas and grows in partial shade as well as full sun. It bears its spikes of white flowers on two to four foot stems in July and August.

GOLDENRODS. (Solidago). The Goldenrods are a large and somewhat bewildering family to a practical wildflower grower who is not much of a botanist. There are over a hundred species of Goldenrods native to North America, and about thirty of them native to New England or New York. While considered somewhat of a hayfield weed by us Americans, yet the Europeans find them a very valuable adjunct to their list of garden plants.

Most of the Goldenrods are easily grown but so easily obtained wild that the wildflower grower may best devote his time to more delicate and unusual flowers.

CANADA GOLDENROD (Solidago canadensis) is a strong-growing variety so common in the Northeast, with stems growing to five feet in height with immense branching heads of golden-yellow flowers in autumn. It is indeed a prominent feature of the landscape and becomes very abundant in neglected upland meadows.

FRAGRANT GOLDENROD (Solidago odora) is indeed a contrast to the giant canadensis. The Fragrant Goldenrod is so called because the leaves when bruised, instead of the usual disagreeable odor of Goldenrod, emit the sweet fragrance of anise. This species grows in thin, poor, acid soil under oaks, but nevertheless appreciates a little care. The plant is nearly evergreen and the medium sized flower heads are borne in late fall.

STARRY CAMPION (Silene stellata). This plant has prettily fringed white flowers in June. It grows about two feet tall in full sun. It is a native of the Atlantic seaboard states.

FLOWERING SPURGE (Euphorbia corollata). Through the late summer the flowers of the Flowering Spurge grow on two foot stems branching after the fashion of cultivated Gypsophila, but it is even better than that plant for use in mixed bouquets because of the stiffer

Disk and Ray-flowers.

GOLDENROD
Solidago lanceolata

stems. It is a native of the sandy lands and open woods of the Central States. It spreads readily from creeping root stalks and may be propagated by means of root cuttings.

ROCK LARKSPUR (Delphinium tricorne) is a delightful little dark blue Delphinium from the Middle States, growing from a peculiar, irregular, fleshy root or bulb to a height of a foot or more and blossoming in late May before any of the cultivated Larkspurs. It propagates easily from seed and succeeds well in open sun or partial shade.

PURPLE CONEFLOWER (Echinacea purpurea). Except for having pink petals, the Purple Coneflower blossoms might be mistaken for the Black-eyed-susan, although it grows taller, reaching a height of three feet. It thrives, however, under similar conditions and bears its flowers liberally from late June until September. This native plant of our prairie states has become a standard species for planting in gardens. Nevertheless, it looks more at home growing along walls and fences. It is propagated from seed.

NARROWLEAF CONEFLOWER (Echinacea angustifolia) is not so showy and attains a height of only about a foot. It is a native of the limestone cliffs and slopes of the Middle West.

WILD HYACINTH (Camassia esculenta). Western America gave us the Wild Hyacinth, which, in the Pacific coast states grew so plentifully that it was a staple product of food with the Indians, but now it has degenerated—or advanced, as you see it—to a place in the garden or natural planting. I have not found it difficult to grow in fairly moist and rich soil. There is no question as to its hardiness in the East, but I do believe it likes to have its roots kept cool during the summer and will grow best among other plants which shade the ground. Stems eighteen to twenty-four inches tall produce flowers varying from cream color to blue and blossom about June first in New England. The variety leichtlini is a taller growing variety and is usually found in deeper colors than the Wild Hyacinth.

PEARL EVERLASTING (Anaphalis margaritacea) is a native of almost all North America and sometimes called a weed, but I wish to protest against this innuendo. There is a touch of the romantic about the Everlastings because they are so closely associated with school days, and have always been on such friendly terms with the boys and girls of the district schools. In early spring we used to pick the blossoms of the Early Everlasting for chewing tobacco, wondering all the time why we could spit bright green juice from chewing snow white flowers.   In late summer we gathered bouquets of the tall Pearl Everlasting to dry for the winter.   That the Pearl Everlasting is not more generally appre-ciated is due solely to the fact that it is so miserably common.

BULB BUTTERCUP (Ranunculus bulbosa).   While the Common Buttercup (Ranunculus acris) reaches a height of three feet and prefers the moist meadows, its little relative, the Bulb Buttercup, grows only about a foot tall, is of compact growth and bears larger flowers during June and July.   As its name implies, it grows from a bulb and might well become a valuable rock plant for sunny locations.

COMMON SHOOTINGSTAR (Dodecatheon meadia) is one of the most delightful contributions of the Central West to the horticultural world.   The pointed flowers, shaped like the head of a dart, are borne in clusters on twelve to fifteen inch stems in late May and early June. They vary in color from white to deep pink.   Although commonly grown from seed I have found that this little wildflower propagates most rapidly from cuttings made in earliest spring before the leaves have started.   In fact, I have had new plants develop from root cuttings in one week's time.

TALL MEADOWRUE
Thalictrum polyganum

CHAPTER XIX

Roadside Neighbors

-)»- -)»- «(- «(-

I WONDER why some wildflowers like human association so much better than others? Is it merely curiosity or just plain friendliness that prompts them to come out of the forest and live by the roadside where they can see and be seen? Sometimes one member of the family, such as the Red Baneberry, will come out to the edge of the road to live, and leave its very close relative, the White Baneberry, which must be much shyer, lingering in the depths of the woods, as if afraid.

No, I am afraid that, much as we would like to think it is love of human company that brings these flowers into closer companionship with people, we must ascribe it to more practical, if less romantic, reasons.

I think they make their home by the roadside for these reasons. The soil is very likely to be rich; the roadsides are nearly always well-drained; and if through a forest these plants also have the benefit of sunshine part of the day and shade the rest. And it is under these conditions that many delightful species seem to thrive best. Of course the roadside where there is most shade is the home of different kinds of plants such as live in the woodlands, but even through the open countryside the tall-growing plants and shrubs provide a certain amount of shade for their little companions.

Fall Asters and Goldenrod delight in roadside conditions, as do innumerable other species, which we are discussing in other chapters.

Unless specifically stated, each species of the roadside plants is best grown from seed.

SPOTTED WATERHEMLOCK (Cicuta maculata) is a great big fellow five to six feet in height and whose hollow branching stem makes him symmetrically broad as well. He grows pretty much over the United States in either sun or shade. The white flowers are borne in compound umbels, three inches or more across, in late summer. Some

83

say the hemlock tea which Socrates drank was made from this plant. It may have been fatal to Socrates, but New England youngsters use the hollow stems for blow guns without disastrous effect.

WILD SARSAPARILLA (Aralia nudicaulis). The yellowish flowers of this plant of the roadside and woods are not conspicuous at blossoming time in May, but the large clusters of blue berries in late summer make it attractive. It grows from twelve to eighteen inches tall.

BRISTLY ARALIA (Aralia hispida) grows along the hot, dry roadsides or railroad embankments. The yellowish flowers in June are not colorful, but its charm lies in the round clusters of blue fruit in autumn. It grows two feet tall.

AMERICAN SPIKENARD (Aralia racemosa) grows to a height of two feet and has greenish white flowers in May, but later in the summer the berries are red. This is a plant for moist shade.

CELANDINE (Chelidonium majus). Originally an immigrant, the Celandine has made itself thoroughly at home on the shaded roadsides of New England. It grows about two feet tall and its Buttercuplike flowers are borne throughout the spring and summer.

TALL MEADOWRUE (Thalictrum polyganum). The lovely, fluffy white flower heads of the Tall Meadowrue on their three to six foot stems from June till September possess an air of stateliness which the coarser flowers blossoming at this time lack. Perhaps it raises its aristocratic head so high to get away from its more plebeian neighbors. The Tall Meadowrue is a native of the bogs and moist ground in either sun or shade, but seems to grow to its best along the moist, shaded wood roads.

EARLY MEADOWRUE (Thalictrum dioicum) grows in the same range as its aristocratic relative, but the misty, purplish flowers are borne in May, and, together with its finely cut glaucous foliage, make the Early Meadowrue one of the delightful flowers of the woods. It attains a height of two feet.

CLOSED GENTIAN (Gentiana andrewsi). The rich, very dark blue, closed blossoms of the Closed or Blind Gentian are a familiar sight along the moist, partially shaded roads of eastern United States and Canada in September. At its best it reaches a height of two feet. It seems to thrive under neutral soil conditions. It is propagated by dividing the plant. There is a pure white form of Gentiana andrewsi, but it is not at all common.

NARROW-LEAVED GENTIAN (Gentiana linearis) is another closed Gentian, which frequents the moist upland meadows and roadsides of northern New England in vast quantities. It apparently is the one member of the family to prefer acid soil. It is often found growing in company with the Lowbush Blueberry. The color is a porcelain blue, sometimes almost white, and it blossoms in mid-July instead of autumn as its relatives do. It is not so tall a grower as Gentiana andrewsi, but a worthwhile wildflower.

ELECAMPANE (Inula helenium). The Elecampane is a large, coarse flower, whose strong, branching, six foot stalks and yellow flowers give it a Sunflowerlike appearance. It is found in the open fields and roadsides of eastern America. It is so large and coarse that it is more likely found in company with shrubs like the Sweetfern and Shining Sumac than with other wildflowers. Of rather picturesque if ungainly appearance, its yellow blossoms do their part to enliven the late summer countryside.

CUCUMBER-ROOT (Medeola virginica) is a cosmopolitan plant of eastern North America, not very particular where it grows as long as it is not too wet, and found in company with Solomonseal, Bunchberry, Trilliums or Arbutus. The Greenish-yellow flowers in May and June are borne on two foot stems. The blossoming plants have two whorls of leaves, one halfway down the stem and the other at the top, which gives it a distinctive appearance. The dark purple berries are quite conspicuous in late summer. The plant gets its name from the white root, about two to three inches long, which is supposed to taste like Cucumbers, but much depends on one's taste.

OSWEGO BEEBALM (Monarda didyma). The brilliant scarlet flower heads of the Oswego or American Beebalm are known in almost all gardens, but it grows wild from New York south to Georgia along the Appalachian Mountains. As its native habitat is along streams one can see that it prefers moist ground. In New England it is found as escapes along the roadsides growing in rather dry soil, but it is at its best in moist shade, sometimes reaching a height of four feet.

This plant with its intense coloring and fragrant leaves is one of the finest for naturalizing under almost any conditions. It spreads rapidly from creeping root stalks and lends its vivid scarlet to the more drab surroundings in August. Do not plant it near Joe-Pye-Weed, as their colors clash.

Single flower.

OSWEGO BEEBALM
Monarda didyma

WILDBERGAMOT (Monarda fistulosa). Although resembling its close relative, the Oswego or American Beebalm, in habit of growth, the Wildbergamot, which is not quite so tall, thrives best in dry, sandy locations. It is plentiful from Ontario south and west. It blossoms from July to September and is pinkish purple or pale lavender.

PURPLE WILDBERGAMOT (Monarda meadia), like the American Beebalm, prefers rich, moist soil and is of similar growth, but the flowers are purplish red.

WOODLAND SUNFLOWER (Helianthus divaricatus) is the most graceful of our wild Sunflowers, growing on slender stems to a height of four to seven feet, and the yellow flowers, about two inches across, are borne on branching stems from July till September. It is a native of the rather dry, shaded roadsides and thickets of eastern America.

WILD SUNFLOWER (Helianthus gigantea) is quite common from the Rocky Mountains eastward to the Atlantic, growing in immense quantities in swamps and marshes along the coast and along the roadsides farther inland. It may reach a height of ten feet and spreads not only from seed, but from creeping root stalks. It is a coarse, picturesque plant with flowers one and a half to three inches broad.

CANDLE ANEMONE or THIMBLEWEED (Anemone cylindrica) is a common roadside Anemone, and the tallest of its family, sometimes reaching a height of nearly three feet. The creamy-white flowers, one to one and a half inches across, blossom in early summer and are followed in late summer by seed pods which burst and display masses which give the youngsters grounds for calling it "Sheep's Wool." This plant prefers full sun or only partial shade.

WOOD MERRYBELLS (Uvularia perfoliata). This native of the rich mountain woods seems to grow to perfection along the partially shaded roadsides. It grows from one to two feet tall and the narrow, drooping, bellshaped flowers of lemon yellow, sometimes two inches long, are borne in early spring. It is one of the most satisfactory wildflowers to grow.

LITTLE MERRYBELLS or BELLWORT (Uvularia sessilifolia) is a miniature relative of the Wood Merrybells, very common in the Atlantic coastal region and inland as far as the Green Mountains of Vermont. The Bellwort grows six to eight inches tall on slender stems, which rise from creeping root stalks, and in very early spring the narrow, drooping, yellowish-white bells are of such appearance that among school children it has acquired the common name of Wild Oats. It is easily grown, a small planting soon becoming quite extensive.

WILD PARSNIP (Zizia aurea). Some might call the Early Meadow Parsnip a weed, but really there is nothing bad about it, so I do not see why any epithet should be applied. Besides, the scientific name, Zizia aurea, in itself makes a delectable swear word. If it were not so very common, and if its yellow blossoms in May were not known to almost everyone, the Early Meadow Parsnip would really be quiet an attractive wildflower. As it is, it is very satisfactory to plant in waste corners or along roadsides.

POTATO BEAN (Apios tuberosa). Clambering over any neighbors who may be convenient, the Potatobean, from the axil of the leaves sends forth clusters of brownish-purple, fragrant, peashaped flowers, which are borne from late July until September. Along its creeping root stalks one finds many fleshy, eggshaped swellings, which I am told are edible, but so far curiosity has not prompted me to prove this statement. But I think the Potatobean is a very useful vine. The top is annual, but the root is very permanent, and new plants may be grown by planting the fleshy tubers on the roots, or from seed. It likes rich, moist soil in which to do its best.

FRINGED LOOSESTRIFE (Steironema ciliatum) is a plant closely allied to the tall growing Lysimachias, but with larger, more separated flowers. It is essentially a plant of the moist thickets and roadsides. From June until August the bright yellow blossoms are borne on slightly branched stems two to three feet tall.

CHAPTER XX

The Glory of the Bogs

-»»- -»»- -«« -««

THE wildflower lover probably makes more interesting discoveries on a trip to the shaded bogs than to any other location. True, he may also discover midgets, black flies and mosquitoes, as well as things that creep and crawl, but nowhere do we find such a wide variety of plant life as we do in the shaded swamps. The moss-covered hummocks, on which trees of Black Ash and Tamarack grow, yield a wealth of color and beauty. Then between the hummocks, where water stands most of the time, another class of native plants may be found, while woodland wildflowers and ferns creep down from the higher, drier places to the very edge of the bog itself. Chainfern, Goldie Fern, Royal Fern and Sensitive Fern may furnish the greenery for Nature's bouquet.

There are some species described in other chapters of this book which are essentially of the bogs. I would mention particularly the Swamp Aster, Wild Marshmarigold, the Showy and Yellow Ladyslippers, Pitcherplants, Joe-pye-weed, Boneset, White and Purple Fringe-orchids, the Twayblades, Meadowrue and several of the Violets.

Bog plants may well be set in either spring or autumn, but if planted in the autumn a light mulch is desirable for the winter. On account of being shaded, the bogs are less likely to thaw out during the winter as do marshes, so there is not the danger of the plants being thrown out of the ground in early spring.

WILD CALLA (Calla palustris). While bogs are inhabited by many things that creep and crawl, yet not all of these are reptiles. One is the Wild Calla. It does not seem right to describe a little plant with such a lovely blossom as creeping and crawling, but I refer to its habit of growth. The Wild Calla is very plentiful in northern New England. The glossy green leaves, roughly heartshaped, grow from four to five inches in length. The blossoms, in midsummer, are true miniature Callas, and are pure white followed by red berries.

89

WILD CALLA
Calla palustris

During the summer the plant sends out a thick, green, creeping root stalk, usually on the surface of the bog, and after it has produced its fruit the old root rots away, leaving this scaly stalk to lie on the ground all winter, with a few white roots along its under surface. The following spring the bud at the end of this adventurous root stalk develops a new plant which in turn will rot away after it has completed its summer's mission. Thus the Wild Calla changes its location by at least a few inches each year. It is sometimes found growing directly out of the water, but usually on beds of slimy muck in the shade. It propagates itself by seed.

WHITE TURTLEHEAD (Chelone glabra). The white flowers of the Turtlehead, so common in bogs and along the moist roadsides in late summer, are found over entire eastern North America. It gets its name Turtlehead from the shape of the flowers, which are white tinged with pink. The plant attains a height of two feet and is propagated by division, a single plant making a large clump in a few years' time.

A deep pink variety, Chelone lyoni, is commonly cultivated in gardens, but this is also adapted to naturalizing and, although both are natives of the swamps, they grow very nicely in quite dry soil.

WHORLED LOOSESTRIFE (Lysimachia quadrifolia) is so called from the position of its leaves, which are borne in sets of four or five the entire length of its two foot stem. The flowers are bright yellow, growing one from the axis of each leaf near the top of the plant. A native of eastern United States and Canada, it grows in almost any bog with shade or partial shade and bears its brightly colored flowers in July.

SWAMPCANDLE (Lysimachia terrestris) is appropriately named because the bright yellow blossoms are borne in candleshaped racemes at the top of the one and a half to two foot stems in late summer.

SWAMP LOOSESTRIFE (Decodon verticillatus) is a tall, purple Loosestrife, more like Lythrum, which grows in the swamps of eastern North America, sometimes reaching a height of several feet, and bearing its clusters of purple flowers close to the stem at the axis of the leaves. The Loosestrifes are all of easy culture and transplant readily.

SWAMP SAXIFRAGE (Saxifraga pennsylvanicum). Imagine Mignonette blossoms growing on three foot hollow stems in the swamps in late May and you have a picture of the Swamp Saxifrage. It grows from rosettes of leaves eight inches across in the mucky ground between the hummocks. It does not seem to have much in common with its little relative, the Mountain Saxifrage, which is only a few inches tall and grows among the rocks at a higher elevation. The Swamp Saxifrage is of very easy culture.

GOLDEN GROUNDSEL or GOLDEN RAGWORT (Senecio aureus). Finding this flower growing wild in the muck of the swamps one would hardly suspect that if transplanted into ordinary garden soil it would prove to be one of the choicest flowers of the entire season.

As I write this, June 1, a patch of Golden Ragwort planted in rather dry, sandy soil is just one shimmering heap of gold. Although the individual flowers are smaller, they are so numerous that the clump presents as gorgeous an appearance as the Helenium does in early autumn. The Golden Ragwort grows to a height of two and a half to three feet and is usually found wild in company with the Purple Avens.

PURPLE AVENS (Geum rivale) is a boon companion of Golden Ragwort in the bogs and a native of most of North America as well as Europe and Asia. The purple, cupshaped flowers are borne on stems about two feet tall, blossoming from late May until into July.

YELLOW AVENS (Geum strictum) is about one foot taller than Purple Avens, with yellow, more open flowers. Both are easy to grow.

SKUNKCABBAGE (Symplocarpus foetida). The Skunkcabbage must be of a sensitive nature. At any rate, it sends its large, curious, hooded, brown flowers up so early in the spring that they are gone by before their outrageous odor can be compared with the fragrance of other spring flowers.

The Skunkcabbage is indeed a freak of Nature, presenting an almost tropical appearance at a time of year when snow banks are still prevalent in the northern woods. The large leaves, sometimes two feet long by one foot across, are borne in dense crowns, but are not much in evidence at the time of blossoming. Although it is claimed that Skunkcabbage is the earliest spring flower, yet we give that honor to the Dwarf Trillium, Trillium nivale. Comparing the Dwarf Trillium with Skunkcabbage is like comparing a Ruby-throated Hummingbird with a Turkey Buzzard, but many consider the Skunkcabbage interesting—at a distance.

AMERICAN FALSE-HELLEBORE (Veratrum viride). When the unfolding green shoots of the Wild Hellebore appear on the hummocks in the bogs one may know that spring is well on its way. As the season progresses, however, and these plants reach their full height of two to five feet with a large, clumsy panicle of green flowers at the top, they lose their attractiveness. But by that time the smaller bog flowers, such as Yellow Ladyslipper, Blue Violet, Ground Raspberry, Avens and Ragwort, use them as a background against which to show their colors of yellow, purple and white. New England bogs would seem very bare indeed without the Wild Hellebore. The roots are supposed to be poisonous, but I understand that the young shoots are sometimes eaten as greens.

GOLDTHREAD (Coptis trifolia). Equally at home in sun or shade, so long as it can grow upon the hummocks of spahgnum moss, the Goldthread gets its name from the rich orange-colored creeping root stalks, by which means it spreads rapidly. The leaves, somewhat like small strawberry leaves, are a rich, glossy green and remain so through most of the winter. The dainty, starry, white flowers are borne on naked stems, which rise from the basal leaves to a height of three or four inches in earliest summer.

AMERICAN GLOBEFLOWER (Trollius laxus) is a rather rare wild-flower growing in the swamps of northeastern United States. It reaches a height of from six inches to two feet and bears yellow flowers about an inch across with centers of golden stamens. This is not a plant for the amateur to expect exceptional success with.

DWARF GINSENG (Panax trifolium). Making itself at home on the hummocks or in the moist, but not wet, soil around the bogs, the tiny Dwarf Ginseng, growing only three to four inches tall, offers its airy, fluffy, white flowers to be admired in early spring. It is one of the most delicate of plants, growing from a bulb, which gives it the common name of Groundnut.

TALL CLUSTER FALSE-DRAGONHEAD (Physostegia speciosa). This grows over a wide range of eastern North America, but does not seem to be very plentiful in any one locality. It has, however, been put under cultivation and is propagated by most nurserymen as it grows so readily from seed or division. A native of the swamps or moist meadows, it nevertheless will grow in almost any type of soil. Its two foot spikes of pink Snapdragonlike flowers in late summer make it one of the best wildflowers for cutting. One may move or blow the blossoms around the stem and they stay wherever they are put, which gives it one of its common names, Obedient Plant.

CARDINALFLOWER
Lobelia cardinalis

CHAPTER XXI

Ponds and Streams

-》》-·》》- 《《-·《《·

A MONG the most picturesque native wildflowers are those that border our ponds and small, running streams. Most of these plants are rather tall growing and blossom late in the season after the beauty of the woodland flowers has disappeared, except for those which bear bright-colored berries.

The plants at the edge of the pond or stream may be divided into two classes: those which grow on the banks and those which grow in the shallow water itself. But in making a natural planting these groups should be considered together. The tall growing ferns are also useful for the border of ponds and brooks, particularly the Ostrich, Cinnamon, Interrupted and Royal Ferns. If the ground is not too wet the Meadow and Turkscap Lilies may well be interplanted.

It is not my intention to tell you here as to the arrangement of plants, for I should surely get myself into trouble. I realize that probably Cardinalflower should not be planted in front of Joe-pye-weed because my volunteer feminine advisers tell me that bright scarlet and dull purple do not make an attractive color combination.

Besides the plants essential to pond and brookside planting which I shall discuss in this chapter, one might well use the Sweetflag, Swamp Milkweed, Wild Marshmarigold, Waterhemlock, Pink Spiraea, Purple Fringe-orchid, Rose Mallow, Cube-seed Iris, Blueflag Iris, Yellowflag Iris, Meadow Lilies, Wild Red Bergamot, Monkeyflower, False Dragonhead, Great Solomonseal, American Burnet, Tall Meadowrue, American Senna, Wild Hellebore, Blue Vervain and Ironweed, using judgment, of course, as to whether the banks of the pond or stream will be suited to any or all of them.

Do not drown a plant that does not want its crown too wet, but

95

many ponds have banks that, while moist, are well drained, and a wide variety of wildflowers and shrubs may well be grown there.

COMMON CATTAIL (Typha latifolia). Of course the waterside plants best known, north, south, east and west are the Cattail, Typha latifolia, and its narrowleaved cousin, Typha angustifolia. These voracious plants make themselves at home in almost any shallow water, so much so that, spreading from their creeping roots, they take possession if permitted to do so.

Jerry Muskrat would be a considerable help in keeping them within bounds if he would confine his menu to them alone, but unfortunately he does not. As a hint to those of my readers who have never been small boys, I will say that the stems of the Cattail flowers make ideal arrows, and I well remember unintentionally placing one with a sharpened nail in the end squarely between two of the upstairs windows of a neighbor's house, farther away that I thought it would reach.

JOE-PYE-WEED (Eupatorium purpureum) is a good-natured lummox willing to grow anywhere for anybody. In fact, Joe does grow wild along roadsides and particularly around ponds and slow running streams from Florida to New Brunswick and west to the prairies. He grows to such a height—sometimes eight to ten feet—that he overshadows almost any other native plant. Fortunately Nature plants him in company with his smaller white-flowered relative and various yellow flowers so that his rather difficult color, a reddish purple, does not clash with them. The Joe-Pye-Weed blossoms in late summer.

BONESET (Eupatorium perfoliatum) is a very close relative of the Joe-pye-weed, but seldom grows over four feet tall and has grayish-white flowers in late summer. In the early days Boneset was always found in the herb closet.

CARDINALFLOWER (Lobelia cardinalis) is probably the most brilliantly colored wildflower. It is of an intense, vivid scarlet. Native along streams and marshes from Canada to Florida and west to the Rocky Mountains, the Cardinalflower is propagated from seed or by dividing the mother plant each year. It is subject to winter killing if conditions are not suited to it. Nature plants it, as a rule, in ground which does not freeze hard. We find that a good way to protect it is by covering it with four or five inches of forest leaves before the ground freezes and removing them in the spring after the danger of severe weather is past. The Cardinalflower is particularly valuable because it blossoms in late summer when bright colors are scarce. It grows from one to three feet tall.

LARGE BLUE LOBELIA (Lobelia syphilitica) is of habit similar to the Cardinalflower, but is bright blue in color. Occasionally white blossoms are found.

TRUE FORGET-ME-NOT (Myosotis scorpioides). The True Forget-me-not is found more commonly on the shores of very small ponds and streams. The variety sold by seedsmen under the name of Myosotis palustris seems to be identical with the wild variety. Many small brooks in New England are lined with the True Forget-me-not, starting from an original planting near the head of the stream, and as pieces of the plants are broken off and washed downstream they lodge against the banks and take root there. It is one of the easiest of all plants to grow and does well in full sun or partial shade.

PICKERELWEED (Pontederia cordata). Pickerelweed, common most everywhere in the shallow waters of the ponds and streams, is likely to take possession if given an opportunity. Only the Cattail seems able to hold its own against it. It spreads from creeping root stalks and has large, glossy leaves extending erect just out of the water and with spikes of blue flowers in midsummer.

COMMON ARROWHEAD (Sagittaria latifolia). Looking at the leaves of this very common water plant it is easy to see where it derives its name Arrowhead. There is a wide variation in the shape of them, however, some being very broad and others quite narrow. Whether they are distinct species or variations in the one species I am not prepared to say. They also vary greatly in height, some dwarf forms only six to eight inches tall being found. They produce their white flowers over a long period in midsummer. It grows best in the muck beside the pond or where the water stands two or three inches deep.

COMMON COLTSFOOT (Tussilago farfara). The masses of large, Dock-like leaves that appear along the wet clay banks and brooksides in late summer are seldom associated with the Dandelion-like flowers which come up all alone in earliest spring. Nevertheless, they are the leaves of the Coltsfoot.

PEPPERMINT (Mentha piperita). Peppermint and Spearmint, having lived in this country since colonial days, ought to be considered native by now. The small running brooks of New England would hardly seem the same if the Peppermint did not grow along them in company with the Coltsfoot and Forget-me-nots. Of course, everyone knows the Peppermint, so we won't describe it, but in planting along the small brook or pond, please include a small patch of it.

SPEARMINT (Mentha spicata). I never smell Spearmint but my mind reverts instantly to the deep holes in the brook where the big trout used to be, and how, in an opening in the woods, there was sort of an island, and standing on this island I would hold the freshly cut fishpole in one hand and with the other pick the young growth of Spearmint to nibble. Sometimes I would catch a trout and then again I might get just a few mosquito bites on my bare legs.

AMERICAN BURNET (Sanguisorba canadensis) is an unusual and picturesque plant found growing naturally to a height of from two to six feet among the stones on the banks of small rivers. The leaves somewhat resemble those of the Pink Spiraea. The creamy white flowers are borne in dense terminal spikes usually four to six inches long. It may be found in bloom from midsummer until autumn and thrives in almost any moist, open location.

AMERICAN LOTUS (Nelumbo lutea) is prominent in ponds from southern New England westward and southward, growing in from two to six feet of water. The almost round, leathery leaves grow a foot or more across and the pale yellow fragrant flowers in August sometimes attain a diameter of eight to ten inches. It seeds freely and may be kept under control to a considerable extent by picking the blossoms. The Lotus grows from tuberous root stalks which are supposedly edible. The pink-flowered form of the American Lotus is frequently cultivated.

SPATTERDOCK (Nuphar advena). Very widely distributed over all America east of the Rocky Mountains, the Spatterdock, or Cowlily, sometimes becomes so rampant as to endanger more delicate water plants. Although usually found growing in shallow water, it sometimes occurs in the muck at the borders of ponds. The bright yellow, globe-shaped flowers are about two inches broad and are borne throughout the summer. Nuphar advena grows from a long, thick root stalk.

AMERICAN WATERLILY (Nymphaea odorata) is common over eastern North America, growing in shallow ponds and sluggish streams from a thick, horizontal root stalk. The leaves grow to twelve inches in diameter and the very fragrant white flowers, three to six inches broad, are produced throughout the summer. In small ponds the White

Waterlily sometimes becomes so numerous that it does not blossom freely.

BITTER NIGHTSHADE (Solanum dulcamara). Originally introduced, but thoroughly naturalized now, the Climbing Nightshade grows plentifully along the wooded banks of our eastern streams or is sometimes found growing by the cellar hole of an abandoned farm where it was planted a hundred years or more ago. The top does not kill back completely each year, but the woody base of the vine seems to be perennial. It grows six to eight feet long over rocks or small bushes, and the rich purple, potatolike blossoms, borne in clusters in June and July, are followed in late summer and autumn by yellow berries which finally become bright red. This plant is not the deadly Nightshade, although it is often called so.

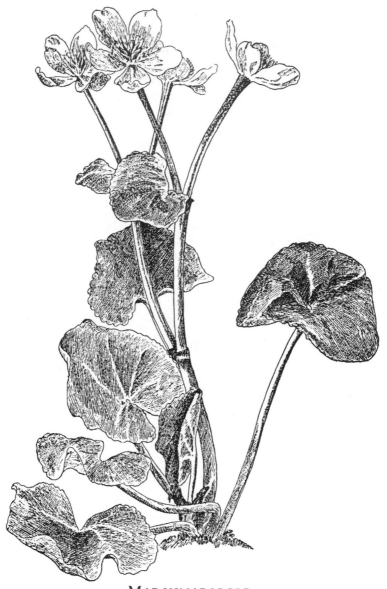

MARSHMARIGOLD
Caltha palustris

CHAPTER XXII

Plants for the Marshes

-»»-»» «-«-

B Y a marsh I mean open, sunny, swampy ground where water stands close to the surface of the soil the year around, and where there is usually a rich growth of grasses and sedges among which the more colorful plants make their home.

Although we have bog gardens, desert gardens, rock gardens, water gardens and innumerable other kinds of gardens, we do not make marsh gardens—not very much anyway. Fortunately we do not have to emulate Nature in this respect in order to grow certain species, for nearly all of her marsh plants grow satisfactorily in almost any good, rich, moist soil, often much more satisfactorily than they do in their native haunts. The plants which I shall describe in this chapter will not include those which are essentially called "bog plants," and which grow on hummocks in the shaded bogs, although it is true that many bog plants grow in the marshes and marsh plants in the bogs.

While the wildflowers described in this chapter may be taken as a basis for a marsh planting, one should not forget that there are dozens of other species also growing in our native marshes, many of which are described in this book. I would name particularly the Pogonia, Calopogon, Ladies-tresses, several of the Violets, Wild Hellebore, Cattail, Meadowrue, Golden Ragwort, Common Pitcherplant, Swamp Saxifrage, False Dragonhead, Loosestrife, Fringed Gentian, Joe-pye-weed and Boneset, White Ladyslipper, Turtlehead and several of the ferns such as Crested Woodfern, Marshfern, New York Fern, Royal Fern, Sensitive Fern and Cinnamon Fern.

Spring is probably the best time to plant a marsh, as far as possible. This is not because the plants are not perfectly hardy, for most of them could be planted in drier soil equally well in spring or fall, but there is a tendency, unless they are well protected, for the frost to throw the newly set plants out on top of the ground in early spring, so when

101

planting the marshes in the fall be sure to give them a mulch, preferably of marsh hay, just before the ground freezes.

SWEETFLAG (Acorus calamus). The broad, grasslike leaves grow to a height of two feet and the blossom is in the form of a spadix completely covered with minute, brownish-yellow flowers. Both the blossoms and the tender growth of the inner leaves are, or were in my school days, readily eaten by children, while the thick, fleshy, creeping root stalk, by means of which the plant spreads, is the source of candied Sweetflag root.

The flowers of the Sweetflag are not showy, but a patch of its light green leaves at the edge of the bog or marsh lends atmosphere to the surroundings.

SWAMP MILKWEED (Asclepias incarnata). This swamp relative of the Butterflyweed is almost as gorgeous, with its large umbels of purple flowers borne in July and August. The plant grows to a height of three to four feet, often in company with Joe-pye-weed, for which it might be mistaken, but the Swamp Milkweed is brighter colored than Joe. Propagation is from seed or division.

MARSHMARIGOLD (Caltha palustris). "The Wild Marshmarigold gleams like fire in swamps and hollows gay." The Cowslip or Marshmarigold, growing in sunny or shaded swamps over most of the eastern United States and Canada, is a veritable blaze of golden yellow, sometimes covering acres. No plant can compare with it.

Although it is probably unnecessary to enlighten any of my readers, I will say that it grows to a height of about a foot and blossoms in early May. The young plants are used as greens for the table. The Marshmarigold propagates readily from seed and is easily transplanted into any soil that is not too dry.

WILD SENNA (Cassia marilandica) is a shrubby, bushy plant from the Atlantic seaboard, growing three to six feet tall and bearing large racemes of orange-yellow flowers in late summer. It is very easily propagated from seed and makes itself at home even in dry, sandy soil. This large-growing plant should not be set near more fragile species.

ROSE LOOSESTRIFE (Lythrum salicaria roseum). Although originally introduced from Europe, the Rose Loosestrife has become thoroughly naturalized in the United States. It is one of the easiest of all flowers to grow, attaining a height of two to three feet, and bearing a profusion of pinkish purple flowers on its tall spikes in July and August. It is grown from seed.

ALLEGHENY MONKEYFLOWER (Mimulus ringens). Growing on stems one to two feet tall, the grinning, Snapdragonlike flowers of clear blue, blossom one or two at a time on the flower spikes in midsummer.

SKULLCAP (Scutellaria integrifolia) is somewhat similar to the Monkeyflower, growing about the same height and bearing its lipped, blue flowers at the axils of the leaves throughout the summer.

CAROLINA PARNASSIA (Parnassia caroliniana). The naked flower stalk rises about a foot above neat tufts of roundish, pale green leaves in late summer. The Anemonelike flowers average a little more than an inch across and are white with green veining. Carolina Parnassia is grown from seed or by dividing the plants, and should be more extensively used. Although a native of the open swamps, it will grow almost equally well in moist, partial shade in the garden border or even in rock gardens if it can be assured of plenty of moisture through its blossoming season. It is a native of eastern North America, south to Virginia and west to Illinois.

BLUE VERVAIN (Verbena hastata). On raised hummocks in the marshes the Blue Vervain is very much at home. Its slender, panicled spikes of royal purple, rising to a height of three feet, from July to September, add their rich coloring to the season. Blue Vervain is desirable for roadside planting in full sun or partial shade and will do its share in the wild garden over a wide range, because it grows naturally from Canada south to Florida and west to Arizona.

TALL IRONWEED (Vernonia altissima). This plant of the lowlands grows considerably taller than the Vervain, sometimes reaching a height of seven to eight feet, and bearing at the top of the stem clusters of thirty to forty fluffy, purple flowers a half-inch or more in diameter. Ironweed grows wild principally in the East Central States, hence it is perfectly hardy, but in planting with other flowers its height should be taken into consideration.

COMMON MEADOWBEAUTY (Rhexia virginica). Growing generally over eastern United States, but not very abundantly except in certain localities, the Meadowbeauty or Deergrass should be considered in making a marsh planting. The flowers are bright purple, about an inch across, and borne from July till September in terminal clusters on square stems twelve to eighteen inches tall. For best results Meadow-beauty should be planted in quantity.

COMMON ROSEMALLOW (Hibiscus moscheutos). Although a native of the marshes along the ocean and the shores of the Great Lakes, Common Rosemallow is perfectly adapted not only to our upland marshes, but it is also widely planted in cultivated gardens. The heavy, thick stalks rise to a height of three to five feet and produce immense, rose-pink flowers six inches across, which cluster at the top of the plant. This gorgeous wildflower is grown easily from seed and the plants increase in size until the third or fourth year. It should have plenty of room in which to develop.

BLUEFLAG IRIS (Iris versicolor). A cosmopolitan Iris that is surely indispensable for a marsh planting. This wild Iris of entire eastern North America blossoms throughout the month of June in New England, and is one of our native plants that will grow with its roots covered with water throughout most of the year. It will also grow in fairly dry locations. Although it seems hardly necessary to tell any-one, I will say that it grows two to three feet tall with Violet-blue blossoms two to three inches across. It is equally at home in sun or shade. Propagation is by seed or division.

CUBESEED IRIS (Iris prismatica) is sometimes called the Narrow-leaved Blueflag because of its slender, narrow foliage and stems, but derives its common name from the shape of the seeds. This Iris will grow either in the water or in dry, sandy soil, although it naturally prefers much moisture. The flat blue flowers on slender stalks give it a graceful bearing.

YELLOWFLAG IRIS (Iris pseudacorus), which comes to us from the far Southwest, is very extensively used in gardens and for natural effect. It is easily grown either with its feet in the water or in a lighter, drier soil. The bright yellow flowers, blossoming in June with the cultivated Siberian Iris, are often erroneously called Yellow Siberian. It is a fine variety for marsh or brookside planting.

CREEPING BUTTERCUP (Ranunculus repens) is an immigrant which goes wandering around the countrysides of the eastern states. It is not objectionable and naturalizes very readily. In moist ground its full double blossoms grow on stems ten to twelve inches tall.

CHAPTER XXIII

Nature Lays a Carpet

JUST as people sometimes lay carpets of different kinds on a bare floor, so Nature often has a bare space in the woods which she decides to cover. For this purpose she has several kinds of plants which spread from creeping root stalks or runners. Although these plants make seed, one will usually be more successful and save much time in growing them from cuttings. Sometimes he will find these cuttings which he makes are already rooted where the trailing plant has lain upon the ground.

Spring is the best time to make cuttings unless one has a greenhouse where they may be started at any time during the winter. These trailing plants may be propagated in beds of sand and as soon as rooted transferred to pots, or the cuttings may be placed directly in small earthen pots containing half sand and half leafmold.

Some kinds root so readily that if taken early in the season before hot, dry weather comes, they may be planted directly where one wishes them to grow. Of course everyone knows that cuttings should not be permitted to dry out, at least until they become well rooted.

In eastern North America Nature uses not only the many species of plants which I shall discuss in this chapter, but others such as Meadow Anemone, Violets, Trailing Arbutus, Bunchberry, Goldthread, Hepaticas, Dwarf Iris, Canada Mayflower, Bluebeads and Creeping Phlox.

PARTRIDGEBERRY (Mitchella repens). First, let us consider the Partridgeberry, which is a native of all eastern United States, growing under both hardwoods and conifers, and making a dense green carpet lying close to the ground. In June the waxy white, fragrant flowers are invariably borne in pairs, which unite to form one berry a third of an inch long with two calyxes. This two-calyxed, bright red fruit seems quite mysterious to one who does not know the nature of the plant.

105

106

PARTRIDGEBERRY
Mitchella repens

The small, round, evergreen leaves are glossy green. The plant is very easily propagated from either cuttings or rooted layers.

Each autumn many people go to the woods to gather the green leaves and bright red berries of this plant, which, when placed in a bowl containing wet moss, continue to grow throughout the winter. In the spring these stems will often be well rooted in the moss and may be transplanted to grow on if desired.

AMERICAN TWINFLOWER (Linnaea borealis americana). In close company with the Partridgeberry we often find the Twinflower, which is a more adventurous grower, but with less attractive leaves and not so compact a habit. Although the Twinflower makes a very delightful ground cover, its beauty is in its pink, fragrant flowers borne in pairs on slender, three to four inch stems in early summer. Twinflower is a northern plant, growing best in the cold woods in acid soil. It propagates very readily from cuttings made in a mixture of sand and granulated peat.

CREEPING SNOWBERRY (Chiogenes hispidula). At home in the dense, cold, northern woods, the Creeping Snowberry, completely covering a rotten log of spruce or hemlock with its rich evergreen leaves and snow white, wintergreen flavored fruit in late summer, presents one of the most attractive pictures of all Nature. Growing luxuriantly as it does on rotten conifer logs indicates clearly that it must have acid. While it is propagated by means of layers or cuttings, yet it takes root slowly and so far we have been unable to grow strong plants in less than two years' time.

COMMON PIPSISSEWA (Chimaphila umbellata). If this plant were a little more easily grown it would be one of the finest ground covers. The rich, glossy, toothed, evergreen leaves grow on stems from six to eight inches tall and the pinkish white flowers are borne in an umbel about three inches above the cluster of leaves. The plant spreads by means of creeping root stalks.

STRIPED PIPSISSEWA (Chimaphila maculata) has whiter flowers than the preceding variety and the leaves are splotched with white along the midrib, giving a variegated foliage effect. Both the Pipsissewas are usually found in dry woods, often, but not necessarily, under pine trees. But, please remember that, like all other plants which grow in dry soil, when they are transplanted they must not be allowed to dry out until thoroughly rerooted. A mulch of pine needles is a great help in this respect.   Both of the Pipsissewas blossom in mid-summer.

CREEPING DALIBARDA (Dalibarda repens).   This fine little ever-green plant of the northern woods is not nearly as well known as it should be, as it is one of the best for a wildflower gardener to start with.   The roundish leaves and flower stems grow to a height of only three or four inches and the delicate white flowers, somewhat like Hepaticas, but smaller, are not only borne plentifully in June and July. but throughout the summer and fall in lesser numbers.   Creeping Dalibarda increases rapidly by means of runners like strawberries, and makes a nice green glossy carpet in only one year's time.

GALAX (Galax aphylla).   Although a native of the southern Appalachians, the Galax is perfectly hardy far to the North, so long as it can have acid soil and shade.   At home it grows among the Rhodo-dendrons and Azaleas, and literally millions of the thick, round, leathery leaves, which change to a bronzy crimson in the fall, are picked and sold to the florist trade.   The spikes of white blossoms grow twelve inches tall and flower in June in Vermont.   This evergreen ground cover spreads itself very rapidly from runners.

MONEYWORT (Lysimachia nummularia).   Although originally an immigrant, the Moneywort, or Creeping Jenny, has become so thor-oughly naturalized that it is known to nearly everyone as a wildflower. As a ground cover it is thoroughly adapted to either covering dry banks or swampy places, and, although inclined to crowd if planted near weaker growing plants, it adapts itself so readily to any location that we find it very useful.   The single, yellow flowers are borne close to the ground in July.

OCONEE-BELLS (Shortia galacifolia).   Like the Galax, it came to us from the Great Smoky Mountains of North Carolina, and, while not quite so strong a grower, yet it makes itself thoroughly at home in acid shade in New England.   The bellshaped white flowers are borne on six inch stems in May.   The leaves, while turning bright colored in autumn and remaining so throughout the winter, do not have the substance of the Galax leaves, yet they form an attractive feature of the plant.   It is easily propagated by dividing the clumps.

COMMON PERIWINKLE (Vinca minor) is another immigrant, but right at home along the stone walls and even in the woods of eastern

United States. The Common Periwinkle or Blue Myrtle is perhaps the most substantial and attractive of all ground covers for shady places. It grows so very rapidly from runners, which root in as they go, the leaves are so glossy and green and hold their attractiveness through the winter, and the bright blue, flat flowers, three-fourths of an inch across, borne in May, are so profuse that we cannot but consider it one of the best.

BARREN-STRAWBERRY (Waldsteinia fragarioides). If we only had a more attractive common or even scientific name for this plant everyone would soon become better acquainted with it. I first saw it carpeting a patch of woods high up in the Green Mountains in company with the Clintonia borealis. This was in June, and the Waldsteinia was a sheet of golden yellow, strawberrylike blossoms on six to nine inch stems, with light green, shiny, three-parted leaves. I saw it again growing in the open sun along a brook, and I found that it blossomed over a long season of four weeks or more and was one of the most easily transplanted of our native plants, spreading rapidly from underground root stalks. While growing in the mountains in either sun or shade, yet when brought to lower elevations I should assuredly plant it in moist shade with plenty of leafmold.

COMMON MAYAPPLE (Podophyllum peltatum). A ground cover does not necessarily have to lie close to the ground or we should leave the Mayapple out of this group of plants, but even though the umbrella-like leaves, often a foot across, grow on top of stems a foot tall, yet they grow so densely that it is impossible to see the ground through a patch of them. While the Mayapple grows wild most commonly in Central United States, yet it makes itself thoroughly at home in New England, spreading from creeping root stalks and is easily divided and transplanted.

The single, white, fragrant flower, sometimes two inches across, has its beauty concealed by the immense peltated leaf above it. The fruit, an inch or more in diameter, ripening in late summer, is round and yellowish green, edible if one likes the flavor, or rather lack of flavor, and gives the plant the common name of Mayapple, but the foliage and root are said to be poisonous, so confine your gastronomic experiments to the fruit alone.

WINTERGREEN (Gaultheria procumbens). Where the shade is

thin among the red maple or pines, or else on the hummocks around the border of an open bog, one finds patches of the Wintergreen.

Spreading from creeping root stalks, it quickly forms carpets of evergreen leaves, which are dull red when mature. The waxy white, bellshaped blossoms in early summer are followed by scarlet fruit, which does not attain full maturity until a year later. The flavor of the Wintergreen is well known to everyone.

CHAPTER XXIV

Ogres of the Bogs

THE word "wildflowers" instantly brings to one's mind thoughts of something sweet and fragrant and pure, and probably fragile and delicate, but never thoughts expressing horror or cruelty. Nevertheless, no living thing can be more cruel or torture its victims in a more horrible manner than do certain attractive bog plants. I refer to our Pitcherplants, Venus flytrap and Sundews. These are, appropriately enough, natives of the bogs, dark and treacherous places for the children of Mrs. Fly, Mrs. Spider and Mrs. Longlegs. These mothers must be as alert for the care of their youngsters, who may stray into the spahgnum bogs, as our South American mothers, whose children stray into jaguar-infested jungles. For these ogres of the bogs literally live on meat—raw meat. They catch it alive and kill it slowly and cruelly.

There are four common species of Pitcherplants, all having liquids in the bottom of their pitchers, and whatever insect is unfortunate enough to fall into these pits with poisonous lakes at the bottom is doomed to certain death and to have all nourishment in his body absorbed by the voracious plant.

The Pitcherplants grow where it is wet, sometimes in muck, more frequently in spahgnum moss, and occasionally in the wet ground around the borders of ponds. They produce large quantities of seed, which ripens in late summer, and by which means they are propagated.

COMMON PITCHERPLANT (Sarracenia purpurea) is usually found growing in spahgnum moss either in sun or shade. It is a broad, low-spreading plant, growing to fifteen inches across, one of the curiosities of the plant world. The pitchers will sometimes contain a half-pint of liquid. They stay green, or reddish if in the sun, all winter, dying away in the springtime, when new pitchers are produced. The curious, reddish-brown blossoms are borne singly on stems a foot tall during June

111

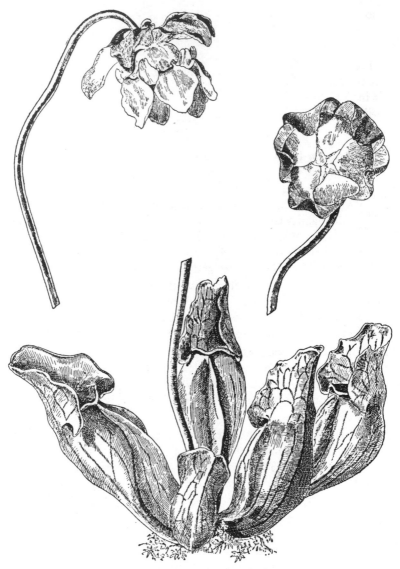

COMMON PITCHERPLANT
Sarracenia purpurea

and July, and the seeds are scattered liberally throughout the moss beds, so that the species is easily perpetuated. This Pitcherplant is often taken into the house for the winter, making an interesting house plant.

The Pitcherplants and the Venus Flytrap are shallow-rooted due to the fact that they receive so much of their nourishment through insects caught in their leaves or pitchers, but when food from the air is scarce they will send their roots deeper in order to secure more from the soil or moss bed.

THE TRUMPET PITCHERPLANT (Sarracenia flava) comes from the Carolinas. Its green pitchers, shaped like trumpets, grow to a height of three feet, while the blossoms are clear yellow. It is perhaps the most easily grown of all the Sarracenias, picturesque to mankind, but deadly to insect life.

THE HOODED PITCHERPLANT (Sarracenia minor) has a really vicious appearance, which should warn bugs to keep away. The end of the leaf is tipped over and downward like the beak of a bird of prey. Possibly the bugs seek shelter here in time of storm, for otherwise there would be no excuse for their getting caught in a trap like this. The Hooded Pitcherplant is really beautiful with its mottled beak formation. The leaves and yellow blossoms both grow about eight inches tall.

SWEET PITCHERPLANT (Sarracenia rubra) is still another species, which is smaller than Sarracenia minor with a similar habit of growth, but the flowers are red instead of yellow. It is apparently the weakest grower of the family.

VENUS FLYTRAP (Dionaea muscipula). For sheer cruelty this plant takes first prize. The open leaves with rows of stiff hair along the edges are a deadly menace to all bugkind. The first time they are touched they stay absolutely motionless, but let Mr. Bug or Worm cross them the second time and the leaves close up with amazing rapidity, spelling the inevitable doom and the assurance of prolonged torture to the victim. They will not open until the last vestige of nourishment has been absorbed from the body of the captive.

Imagine, if you will, the sorrow and agony of the Longlegs family when Daddy Longlegs fails to return some night and the next morning Mrs. Longlegs sets forth to hunt him up, and finds him with his long legs and arms waving frantically in the air and his body fastened securely in the grip of this vicious little plant.

In our small bed of Dionaeas I have often seen several Daddy Longlegs caught at once, all waving their legs frantically and calling for help. The Flytrap, native of the South, should be protected with a mulch of leaves during the winter, so that it will not freeze. It has a white blossom on a six inch stalk in midsummer. The Venus Flytrap is as attractive and interesting to human beings as it is deadly to the insect world.

ROUNDLEAF SUNDEW (Drosera rotundifolia). Tiniest of the ogres, but no less deadly, are the Sundews, of which the Roundleaf Sundew is the most common, growing in the spahgnum of the bogs or on the moist banks of the brook or pond. The tiny leaves, lying flat on the ground, are covered with stiff hairs, which secrete a fluid deadly to bugkind. This fluid first entangles the feet of the insect and then the hairs seize and hold him securely to be devoured at leisure. The white blossoms are borne on very slender six inch stems.

CHAPTER XXV

Fringed Gentian ^{Gentiana crinita}

Gentiana crinita

-»»-»»-«««-«««-

MORE misleading information has probably been distributed regarding the Fringed Gentian than almost any other wildflower. I have even seen it classed as an annual by a supposedly competent authority.

As a matter of fact, Fringed Gentian seems to be one of the easier wildflowers to propagate and grow successfully, but a thorough understanding of its habits and requirements is necessary, for the least variation from the proper procedure in growing it is likely to result in failure.

The Fringed Gentian is a true biennial, and if permitted to make seed will flower but once. A native of moist meadows and marshes of most of northern United States, it nevertheless has been one of our more elusive wildflowers. However, it has now been brought under successful cultivation and the fears in certain circles that it might be exterminated are groundless.

I believe the credit for putting this loveliest of wildflowers on a safe footing should be given to Professor A. S. Kinney of Massachusetts, who, so far as I know, was the first to prove that it could be easily grown in commercial quantities.

The Fringed Gentian blossoms in September and October and ripens its seed within two or three weeks after the blossoms have gone by. The seed should be gathered and sown as soon as ripe in sandy soil containing a small percentage of alkaline humus. Fringed Gentian will not tolerate acid conditions. If it is found impossible to sow the seed immediately it may be kept until spring, but it should be kept moist and in an airtight container. If permitted to dry out it will require an extra year in which to germinate.

After sowing the seed in flats they should be placed where they will be safe from the drip of water. If taken into a greenhouse the young plants will come up thickly in early winter and make considerable size

115

FRINGED GENTIAN
Gentiana crinita

before spring. If the flats are left out-of-doors the seed will not germinate in New England until May, when they seem to come up all at once
so thickly that the ground has the appearance of being covered with a
green mold.

After acquiring some size and strength, the tiny seedlings may be
transplanted into small clay pots or flats. Do not use paper pots for
this purpose, as they do not give satisfaction. The potting soil should
consist mostly of clear, sharp sand with sweet leafmold added as a
fertilizer. The top leafmold of beech and maple trees is best for this
purpose. A few years ago I thought it unsafe to use leafmold, but this
is one thing I have had to revise my opinion on, for the top mold under
beeches and maples seems to be alkaline.

The little seedlings grow very slowly at first, but if given good care
and not permitted to dry out for an instant will make plants two inches
across the first season. They may be planted in their permanent location in September or kept through the winter in cold frames and planted
into the garden or natural location the next spring.

With good care their roots will completely fill two or two and a half
inch pots the second spring and there may be some difficulty, if they
become root-bound, in getting the roots to let go of the sides of the
pot. It is not necessary to plant Fringed Gentian in the open ground,
but they may be carried through their entire life cycle in pots, and after
being given their final transplanting into six inch pots will develop
into strong, heavy plants two feet tall and yield their lovely, fragile,
sky-blue flowers in profusion.

The three cardinal rules to observe in growing the Fringed Gentian
are:

First: Sow the seed as soon as ripe.

Second: Never put them in acid soil.

Third: Do not let them dry out.

To make sure of a supply of seed, watch them closely at blossoming
time and protect them when frosts threaten.

Disk and Ray-flower.

NEW ENGLAND ASTER
Aster Novae-anglia

CHAPTER XXVI

Wild Asters

→»→»←«←«

THE Asters comprise one of the largest families of wildflowers, numbering over two hundred species, but for practical consideration I am limiting the number described here. They are adapted to a wide range of conditions, such as roadside, woodland and swamp planting. They are very easily grown in soil to which they are suited, and should be planted in masses to get the best result. Natural propagation is from seed, but plants with individual characteristics may be readily propagated by division.

Most of our named varieties of cultivated perennial Aster are of novibelgi species, but novae-angliae also produces many shades of vivid and interesting colors.

While wild Asters are more or less subject to blight, yet this is usually due to the fact that soil or other conditions are not suited to that particular species.

BLUE WOOD ASTER (Aster cordifolium) is a roadside species, growing from one to three feet tall, and bearing great masses of small, lilac-colored flowers during September and October. It prefers partial shade.

HEATH ASTER (Aster ericoides) grows from one to two feet tall in the dry land by the roadsides, bearing myriads of white, snowflake-like flowers in autumn.

SWAMP ASTER (Aster puniceus) is a tall-growing species from two to six feet in height, and is sometimes appropriately called the Purple-stemmed Aster. The lavender flowers blossom during the months of August and early September. Although a native of the shaded bogs, the Swamp Aster is a strong, healthy variety for growing in any place where the soil is not too dry.

NEW YORK ASTER (Aster novibelgi) is a species from the open

meadows, in varying shades of blue or violet. This is the Aster from which most of our named garden varieties are selected.

FLAT-TOP ASTER (Aster umbellatus) is a white species, growing usually four to six feet tall in the rather open woodlands and marches, but is sometimes quite plentiful in dry soil. The flowers are borne in very large corymbs from midsummer until late autumn.

NEW ENGLAND ASTER (Aster novae-angliae) is a tall magnificent variety from the open fields, swamps and woodlands. Despite its name, it is found over most of the United States east of the Rocky Mountains, but perhaps most plentifully in New England and New York. It blossoms in September, its rich color varying through all shades of blue and purple to bright pink or reddish. In my opinion it is the most satisfactory of all the Asters, whether wild or cultivated.

NARROWLEAVED ASTER (Aster linnaeafolia) grows from one to two feet tall in dry, sandy soil in most states east of the Mississippi. It has large violet-colored blossoms from midsummer until early autumn.

SEASIDE or SHOWY ASTER (Aster spectabilis), as its name implies, is a large-flowered species, rich purple in color. It grows from one to two feet tall in a dry, sandy soil along the Atlantic coast.

PHILADELPHIA FLEABANE (Erigeron philadelphicum). Because of their Asterlike appearance the Fleabanes may well be considered with them. Philadelphia Fleabane is common throughout most of North America. Its upright panicles of pink, Asterlike flowers, each about three-fourths of an inch across, are borne throughout the summer. It grows two to three feet tall in the fields or open woods.

POOR-ROBINS-PLANTAIN (Erigeron pulchellus) grows from one to two feet tall with flowers of lavender blue about an inch across, borne either singly or several to the stem. Poor-robins-plantain blossoms in New England in June and spreads rather rapidly from creeping root stalks in open land, by roadsides, or in the open woods.

CHAPTER XXVII

A Little Desert

‹‹‹ ‹‹‹ ››› ›››

OUR western plains and semi-desert localities have a fascination for everyone and it is only natural that easterners have a desire to grow the plants which are found there.

I find that most of these plants are not difficult to handle in our eastern location provided one is careful in selecting the place where they are to be set, or, if one has no spot adapted to growing them, to use care in the preparation of a miniature desert.

Semi-desert land does not mean that the soil is not fertile, for all plants require nourishment. In preparing a spot to grow Cacti and other plants of the arid sections, one should first consider drainage. This must be perfect, for any place where water would stand at all in autumn would keep these plants growing so late that winter injury would result. Therefore, a sandy, rocky location with good loam and some leafmold added is desirable. On the top of the soil there should be gravel or coarse sand to prevent mud from sticking to the base of the plants.

In their native homes the semi-desert plants are accustomed to intense heat in the summer and cold in the winter. After a hard winter Cacti may look as if they had shriveled beyond any hope of recovery, but the warm days and rains of spring revive them amazingly, and by June they will be found making new growth for the year.

OPUNTIA VULGARIS is the eastern Cactus, a member of the Pricklypear family with few spines, found growing on the cliffs and dry, gravelly locations as far east as southern New England. It is very easy to succeed with and the leaves or joints broken off and stuck in the soil root readily. It has yellow blossoms in July.

BRITTLE CACTUS (Opuntia fragilis) is a little spiny Pricklypear, whose leaves or joints are only about an inch in length. It increases quite rapidly and is a satisfactory variety.

121

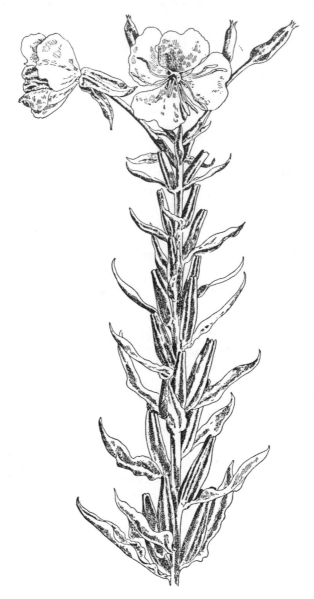

EVENING-PRIMROSE
Oenothera speciosa

OPUNTIA POLYACANTHA, the Pricklypear of the plains, whose large joints thickly set with sharp spines are so common with our western friends. So far as I can see it is no trouble at all to grow them in the East in light, sandy soil. They have large yellow blossoms in midsummer.

CORYPANTHA VIVIPARA is a small round Cactus only a couple inches across, which increases in number slowly from offshoots. It appears to be perfectly hardy with us. Plowing the prairie land for agricultural purposes has reduced its numbers so that it is not very easy to get.

DWARF BLUEBELL (Campanula pumila). A tiny little Bluebell which came to us from South Dakota. It grows only two to three inches tall and the little blossoms resemble those of the Bluebells of Scotland. It makes itself at home in hot dry places and increases quite rapidly by dividing the plants.

SOAPWEED YUCCA (Yucca glauca) is the common Soaproot of the western plains, whose heavy spikes of greenish white flowers rise to a height of two to three feet.

EVENING-PRIMROSE (Oenothera speciosa). One who has seen acres of the Evening-primrose in bloom on the plains will have a permanent affection for this plant. The plant itself is not very attractive, but rather sprawling and semi-prostrate. The white cup-shaped flowers, two inches across, with green markings at the center are borne over a long season in June and July. To do its best it should have dry soil and lots of sunshine.

TUFTED EVENING-PRIMROSE (Oenothera caespitosa) has even larger flowers than the white Evening-primrose. Its blossoms have a tendency to change to rose color as they age.

SHELL-LEAF PENSTEMON (Penstemon grandiflorus). It is hard to see why such an especially beautiful wildflower has escaped being generally introduced into all gardens. This Penstemon, so far as I know, is easily the best of the entire family. It grows wild in the hot, sandy soil of the Dakotas, where it is subjected to extreme heat in summer and extreme cold in winter. The leaves are broad and very glaucous and grow to the top of the eighteen inch stems. The tubular blossoms, borne at the axils of the leaves, are as large as flowers of the cultivated Foxglove and of a delightful lavender blue color. In June this Penstemon of the hot, sandy soil vies with the Showy Ladyslipper of the bogs in attracting attention among wildflowers.

STARLILY (Leucocrinum montanum) is a tiny, Lilylike plant from the Rocky Mountains, whose fragrant white flower clusters are borne in early spring on stems a few inches tall. It does nicely in the East when planted in light, sandy soil, and propagates rapidly by dividing the clumps.

BITTERROOT (Lewisia rediviva) does not object at all to being grown in eastern gardens provided the soil is hot enough and poor enough. The plant dries up and practically disappears during the summer, but in autumn, when rains and cooler weather have come, sends forth its narrow, evergreen leaves and in early summer the large pale pink or white blossoms look very much like Waterlilies sitting on the sand.

CHAPTER XXVIII

Ferns

BECAUSE the hardy ferns grow on such intimate terms with the wildflowers and are almost invariably used in making a wild garden, it seems appropriate to conclude this book with a chapter on them.

There are species which will grow luxuriantly in almost every conceivable location except where it is too hot and sandy—tiny little fellows for clefts in the ledges or in the very forefront of a woodland planting, giant species several feet tall that grow on the borders of ponds and along the brooksides, evergreen kinds of the forest, with which has been developed the commercial industry employing hundreds of people, ferns of the bogs and the marshes, and finally species that grow on the hot hillsides or in seams of granite boulders exposed to the burning midsummer sun.

Ferns are of special value for planting on the shady side of buildings to enhance the beauty of Rhododendrons and Laurel.

The tall growing species may be used as a background for a planting of wildflowers.

Several species thrive in indoor culture. Most prominent of these is the Christmas Fern, and an indoor wildflower garden or terrarium would hardly be complete without some tiny Spleenwort, Oakfern or Walking Fern.

Ferns may be planted at almost any time when the ground is not frozen, but if set out in the summer when they are in growth, I find it advisable to cut them back to the ground. They will invariably start into growth again, although the new fronds will not be so tall or vigorous as those from plants transplanted when dormant.

The depth to which ferns should be planted varies according to the species. Large ferns, such as the Ostrich Fern, the Osmundas and Braun's Hollyfern, prefer to have the top of their crowns above the surface of the soil. Species with creeping root stalks, such as Marshfern, Hay-scented Fern and Climbing Fern, move nicely as sods. These sods should be planted level with the surface of the ground. The little rock ferns, like Maidenhair Spleenwort, should be set with crowns even with the surface. The Common Polypody grows in sheets on ledges and boulders and parts of these sheets may be cut off and moved to new locations, but care should be taken to press them down firmly in their new home and keep them thoroughly wet until they have reestablished themselves. Small species with creeping root stalks, like Beechferns and the Oakfern should have these root stalks planted about two inches below the surface.

It seems immaterial to most ferns whether the soil they are planted in is neutral or moderately acid. The Chainfern and Climbing Fern, however, apparently insist upon very acid soil conditions. Nearly all species appreciate a liberal allowance of leafmold.

Ferns propagate naturally from spores and creeping root stalks. A few have peculiar methods of increasing their number, which will be described as we discuss the species separately.

AMERICAN MAIDENHAIR (Adiantum pedatum). Graceful in the extreme, the Maidenhair Fern with its wiry black stems and light green foliage attains a height of two feet on the rich sloping hillsides in the shade of maples and birches. It is scarcely ever found in poor soil.

Leafmold seems essential to the welfare of the Maidenhair, and if granulated peat is used as a substitute I would recommend that its acidity be diluted or neutralized by the use of some alkali such as wood ashes. The Maidenhair is propagated from seed and to some extent by division of the slowly creeping root stalks. It may be grown alone in masses, but preferably in conjunction with other plants such as Jack-in-the-pulpit, Sharplobe Hepatica, Baneberries, Evergreen Woodfern and other ferns.

EBONY SPLEENWORT (Asplenium platyneuron). I think this grows to its best in the open glades in the rich hardwoods, and its erect, narrow, upright fronds with dark stems average six to ten inches in height, but occasionally grow to eighteen inches or more. The Ebony Spleenwort also grows in the pockets of shelving rocks where leafmold and pulverized stone of centuries has accumulated. It should not be planted where it is too wet, but should be in soil which retains moisture. It is grown without difficulty from spores, which ripen in late summer. The first year the fronds lie flat on the ground, but the next year grow bolt upright.

MAIDENHAIR SPLEENWORT (Asplenium trichomanes). Only the Harebell can root as securely in the crevice of a ledge as the Maidenhair Spleenwort. This tiny, dainty fern is perhaps the finest of all rock ferns. It grows wild where it is almost impossible to dig it, but is one of the most easily propagated in captivity. The tiny plants, only three to four inches tall, may be divided each year and if grown where the soil is moist, but not wet, have a tendency to increase naturally by means of spores.

LADY FERN (Athyrium filixfemina) is a graceful, all-around species preferring partial shade, but also growing along open roadsides and fences. The Lady Fern attains a height of two to three feet and is one of the best ferns for a beginner to grow or to plant in a doubtful location. It has a reclining root stalk, which should be planted just below the surface.

NARROWLEAF SPLEENWORT (Athyrium pycnocarpon) grows in the rich woods and sometimes on the hummocks in the bogs in company with the Crested Woodfern. It is perhaps the cleanest looking fern we have. It grows two feet tall with wavy light green pinnae. Like the Lady Fern, it grows from a shallow, slowly creeping root stalk, and, although not common in the wild, will adapt itself to almost any rich, shady location such as will grow Trilliums, Maidenhair Fern and Jack-in-the-pulpit.

SILVERY SPLEENWORT (Athyrium thelypteroides) resembles the Lady Fern very closely in size and habit of growth, but in late summer the fruit dots on the under side of the fronds are silvery in color whereas those of the Lady Fern are brown. These two species grow together very commonly.

GRAPEFERNS (Botrychium). While there are half a dozen species of Grapeferns and several more varieties, yet only two are of general interest for natural planting, the others being of value principally to collectors and scientists.

The Grapeferns get their name from the fancied resemblance of the clusters of sporangia or fruit spores to a bunch of grapes.

RATTLESNAKE FERN (Botrychium virginianum) grows from a cluster of short, fleshy roots. It is found in the open hardwoods, often in rather poor soil, and attains a height of eighteen inches.

TERNATE GRAPEFERN (Botrychium obliquum) grows in poor soil in the pastures and open woods and attains a height of ten to twelve inches. The fruiting stalks of the Ternate Grapefern grow from the ground instead of on the same stalk as the fronds, as in the case of the Rattlesnake Fern. The Ternate Grapefern peculiarly stays green throughout the winter and dies down in springtime. By midsummer, however, new leaves and the fruiting stalks are produced by the heretofore dormant plants. Propagation of the Grapeferns is invariably from spores.

WALKING FERN (Camptosorus rhizophyllus). A peculiar little evergreen species with leathery, tapering fronds from six to twelve inches long, which produces so-called "feet" at the apex of the frond. This "foot" takes root and furnishes a new plant, and the Walking Fern propagates so rapidly by this means that a few plants set in congenial soil may form a solid mat in one season's time.

Although not a very common fern, it is one of the very easiest to grow, the one essential requirement being dense shade. Many believe that the Walking Fern will grow in alkaline soil only, but this is not the case, as it thrives wonderfully well under rich, acid conditions.

It is essentially a rock fern, and grows naturally on limestone cliffs, although the material on which it grows is not necessarily alkaline.

HARTSTONGUE (Scolopendrium vulgare). The Hartstongue Fern, although rare in the United States, is found very plentifully in the British Isles, and the thick, leathery fronds, not over two inches wide but sometimes eighteen inches long, make it a very distinctive species for a rockery planting. It is claimed that this is about the easiest of all fern species to propagate from spores.

BERRY BLADDERFERN (Cystopteris bulbifera). This fern grows to perfection along the rocky banks of a small brook where it may at times be wet by the spray, and the long, tapering fronds, sometimes nearly three feet in length, make it one of the most graceful of all the ferns. It is propagated most easily by means of small bulblets, which form on the under side of the fronds. When mature these bulblets fall to the ground and if covered very lightly and kept moist will immediately form new plants.

BRITTLE FERN (Cystopteris fragilis). Even after one becomes fairly familiar with the Brittle Fern he may still continue to confuse it with the Obtuse Woodsia. The Brittle Fern is very common on our wooded New England hillsides where the soil is rich and there is plenty of moisture. It is a very delicate fern, attaining a height of not over twelve inches, but is easily grown in the shaded rock garden or any place where a low growing, fragile species is desired.

HAY-SCENTED FERN (Dennstedtia punctilobula). If in doubt as to your ability to grow ferns, experiment with the Hay-scented, for it is one of the very easiest of all to succeed with. It grows from one to two feet tall and forms dense mats of graceful, light green fronds, which, when crushed, emit the fragrance of new mown hay. The hillside pastures of New England, south and westward have many beautiful carpets of this species, and it also grows in the open shade. Sometimes a wide seam of a ledge or boulder will be completely filled by the Hay-scented Fern. It is usually possible to move this in sods a foot square, and very quick results may be obtained by this method. It spreads from creeping root stalks and the number of plants may be increased very rapidly.

CRESTED WOODFERN (Dryopteris cristata). Almost always found on the hummocks in the bogs, the Crested Woodfern with its almost evergreen fronds is one of the most beautiful species. It grows twelve to sixteen inches in height and is often found in company with the Narrowleaf Spleenwort.

CLINTON WOODFERN (Dryopteris clintoniana) is of similar appearance to the Crested Woodfern, except being larger in every way, growing to a height of two feet or more. Both the Crested and Clinton Woodfern take kindly to cultivation, increasing in size and beauty when planted in rich, moist earth.

GOLDIE FERN (Dryopteris goldiana) is indeed the largest of all the so-called Woodferns, growing to four feet in height and quite easily identified by the stems, which are very chaffy at the base. Goldie Fern produces offshoots from the mother crown, which, when separated and transplanted, will in one season's time make as large a crown as the one from which they were removed. In some sections Goldie Fern is protected by law, but the ease with which it is propagated should make it available to all who desire it. Goldie Fern is nearly but not quite evergreen, its fronds retaining their attractiveness until very late in the fall.

NARROW BEECHFERN (Dryopteris phegopteris). In the moist woods or along a brook where shade is quite dense one will find limitless numbers of the Narrow Beechfern, often in company with the Oakfern. When put under cultivation the Narrow Beechfern spreads quite freely from slender creeping root stalks, sending up one frond in a place to a height of about six inches.

WINGED WOODFERN (Dryopteris hexagonoptera), often called Broad Beechfern, is found in drier, more open soil than its narrowleaved relative, and grows to a considerably larger size, sometimes nearly a foot broad. It is invariably broader than it is long, and the two lower pinnae are tilted in such position that it seems as if this fern were continually getting ready to "take off."

Although I had considerable difficulty in locating my propagating stock, and finally found it only a few hundred yards in the dry woods back of my office, yet it is increasing so rapidly from its creeping roots that there seems to be no liklihood of being without it again.

OAKFERN (Dryopteris linnaeana), a tiny fern only a few inches tall with triangular fronds three to six inches long and equally broad. Like the Beechferns, it spreads from its wiry, creeping root stalks, which send up here and there new fronds all summer long. The older ones turning dark green and the new ones being pale green give a patch of this fern a variegated appearance. It is a delightful little species for any shaded situation where a fern so delicate and fragile can be used. Growing wild it seems to associate pretty generally with the Narrow Beechfern.

MARSHFERN (Dryopteris thelypteris) forms thick patches of fronds averaging a foot tall in marshy meadows and along moist roadsides.

NEW YORK FERN (Dryopteris noveboracensis) grows about the same size as the Marshfern, but the fronds are widest at the middle, tapering at both ends. It is likely to be found in drier soil than the Marshfern and also prefers more shade.

LEATHER WOODFERN or EVERGREEN WOODFERN (Dryopteris marginalis) is indispensable for a woodland planting, for the perfectly formed, evergreen, leathery fronds, from one to two and a half feet long are one of the most attractive features of the forest throughout the year. It grows in the rich, rocky woodlands, reproducing readily from spores and growing usually in company with the Christmas Fern and the Maidenhair Fern.

TOOTHED WOODFERN (Dryopteris spinulosa) is almost, but not quite, evergreen, with fronds from eighteen to thirty inches long and growing in the rich, rocky, moist woodlands.

The variety of this fern, Dryopteris spinulosa intermedia, is known as the Fancy Fern and is literally picked by millions for the florist trade each year.

Some people are apprehensive that continued picking will destroy this fern, but one should remember that the fronds are mature and ready to die anyway when they are picked, and I cannot see that any great damage has been done to this variety as yet.

HARTFORD or CLIMBING FERN (Lygodium palmatum). A few years ago the Climbing Fern or Hartford Fern was thought to be nearly extinct, but a large supply was found just in time to save it from being plowed under by a New England farmer, and there seems to be no further danger of losing this unique species.

The Climbing Fern grows in thickets or pastures where it can find Wild Spiraeas, Blueberry, or other shrubs to clamber upon. The sterile fronds, which come up first in the spring, attain a height of only a few inches, but in midsummer the fertile fronds, which are infinitely more graceful, start and grow as tall as three or four feet.

I find that the Climbing Fern is most easily increased by division of the creeping root stalks. Although advised that it was necessary to move this fern in sods to be successful, this did not prove to be the case, as even small pieces of the root form new plants. The Climbing Fern seems to be one of few plants that absolutely insist upon very acid soil.

SENSITIVE FERN (Onoclea sensibilis), sensitive to frosts, but not sensitive about hurting the farmer's feelings, because the broad fronds will sometimes take possession of his hayfield. However, when the Sensitive Fern takes charge of the fields it is an indication that they need plowing and fertilizing.

In the swamps, even where it is almost in the water, the Sensitive Fern is magnificent, growing to nearly three feet in height and giving a most tropical appearance to the vicinity. It spreads from creeping root stalks, although it produces clusters of berries, which contain its spores. Unlike other ferns, the Sensitive Fern does not discharge its spores until the following spring.

COMMON ADDERSTONGUE (Ophioglossum vulgatum). A quaint little fern, which grows from a fleshy root stalk to a height of six to ten inches, with a frond which resembles a leaf halfway up the stalk and a spore cluster at the top, so shaped as to give this fern its common name of Adderstongue.

The Adderstongue has been considered very rare, but it is rare in the same sense that four-leaf clovers are rare. If one visits the marshes and bogs and sits down and waits patiently he is likely to soon begun to see the Adderstongue, but a hasty search for it is usually unavailing.

I have found it growing plentifully in alkaline bogs with the Fringed Gentian, in acid bogs with the Pitcherplant, and also on dry, shaded hillsides where hardly anyone would think of looking for it. It is propagated from spores only.

CINNAMON FERN (Osmunda cinnamomea). One of the giant ferns, growing three to six feet in height, a native of bogs, meadows, open woodlands and roadsides, and one of the most easily grown of all species. In early spring, while the conspicuous fronds, known as "fiddleheads," unfold, the fertile fronds, bearing the spores, spring up hastily to become developed before the rich green, gigantic leaves overtake and envelop their growth. The fertile fronds die down in early summer, but the leafy fronds retain their charms until early fall.

INTERRUPTED FERN (Osmunda claytoniana), which grows even larger than the Cinnamon Fern, differs from the Cinnamon Fern in the manner of producing its spores, the fruit spores being produced on the middle section of the leafy fronds, giving this species the common name of Interrupted Fern.

To those who have difficulty in distinguishing the leaf fronds of the Cinnamon Fern from the sterile fronds of the Interrupted Fern, I will say that at the base of each pinna on the Cinnamon Fern will be found a small tuft of wool. This is entirely lacking on the Interrupted Fern. Both these species are very long lived and substantial. Digging the plants is usually accomplished by means of an axe, as a spade makes little impression on the extremely tough mat of roots with which the crowns are surrounded.

ROYAL FERN (Osmunda regalis) is often called the Flowering Fern. It grows either on the moist, open hillsides or in the shaded bogs.

Like the Sensitive Fern, the Royal Fern attains a much larger size when grown with its root almost in the water. The unfolding fronds in early spring are almost wine colored, and from the time they start growth until the mature plant dies down in autumn are a picture of grace and beauty.

As a clump of Royal Fern increases in age new plants are formed in a perfect circle, sometimes two feet across. What the reason for this geometrical precision is, I cannot say, but the fact remains that, particularly on the open hillsides, a family of Royal Ferns is invariably found growing in this manner. The fronds are twelve to fifteen inches broad and attain a height of three to five feet.

COMMON POLYPODY (Polypodium vulgare) is a small, leathery, evergreen fern six to eight inches tall almost invariably growing on rocks or ledges, but nevertheless may be transplanted into rich, moist soil for purposes of propagation. It spreads into such dense mats by creeping roots, which intertwine, that sections may be cut away and moved to new locations. But in transplanting it be sure that it is pressed firmly onto the ledge or rock where it is to grow and not permitted to dry out until it has become established.

CHRISTMAS FERN (Polystichum acrostichoides), so called because of its generous use as a decoration at Christmas time. With the advent of cold storage it is used by florists the year around, although not so generally as the Fancy Fern (Dryopteris spinulosa intermedia).

Christmas Fern, which is also called Sword Fern and, commercially, Dagger Fern, may be grown successfully indoors during the winter. One finds it wild in rich, rocky woods, usually with Maidenhair and Evergreen Woodfern, and perhaps the Woodsias and Brittle Fern or Spleenworts, growing nearby. It is propagated by spores and is easily established.

BRAUN HOLLYFERN (Polystichum brauni). In most parts of North America Braun Hollyfern is very rare, but in certain sections it seems to grow as plentifully as almost any species. The fronds, which taper at each end, and grow two feet long, may be identified by the great amount of chaff along the stem.

In planting this unusual fern it is well to leave a considerable part of the crown extending above the surface as it grows that way naturally. Another thing to remember is that much sunlight will likely prove fatal to this species, as it grows invariably in rich, dense shade.

BRACKEN (Pteridium aquilinum). The Bracken or Eagle Fern is found on dry hillsides and in open woods pretty much over eastern North America. It is a very easily satisfied fern of rather coarse texture, growing two to three feet tall from creeping root stalks, and its saving feature is that it will grow in places where other ferns refuse to be happy.

OSTRICH FERN (Pteretis nodulosa). "Graceful giant" describes the Ostrich Fern, for along the banks of the rivers and brooks where alluvial soil has been deposited it grows to a height of five to seven feet. Back on the hills in sun or shade one rarely finds it over four feet in height.

A choice companion for the Ostrich Fern is the Meadow Lily, which has to exert itself to much more than its normal growth in order that its flowers in July may show just above the tops of the ferns.

The Ostrich Fern grows with the top of the crown out of the soil and should be planted that way. It propagates from spores, also from underground root stalks or runners. It is ideal for planting on the shady side of a building and along ponds and streams. Its only unfortunate characteristic is that the fronds die down in late August, much earlier than those of the Osmundas.

COMMON WOODSIA (Woodsia obtusa), or Blunt-lobed Woodsia, is a delicate fern species from the rocky woods. It likes rich soil, is often confused with the Brittle Fern and grows from eight to fifteen inches in height.

RUSTY WOODSIA (Woodsia ilvensis). A broad seam in a granite ledge exposed to the full heat of the summer sun makes a perfect home for the Rusty Woodsia. Where no other fern, with the possible exception of the Hay-scented, would even consider growing, the Rusty Woodsia thrives beautifully, growing only six to eight inches tall. Its root stalks and fronds are covered with scales, which turn brown with age, giving the plant a rusty appearance and its name.

NARROWLEAF CHAINFERN (Woodwardia areolata) is a native of the swampy woods. The sterile fronds are nearly a foot tall, and fertile fronds about twice that height. It is not a common species, but is found quite plentifully in the Middle Atlantic States and more sparingly elsewhere along the coast.

VIRGINIA CHAINFERN (Woodwardia virginica) is commonly found in swamps and bogs along the Atlantic coast. The sterile fronds resemble small fronds of the Cinnamon Fern. The Chainferns grow from tough creeping root stalks, often in spahgnum moss or the muck of the bogs, indicating clearly that they require an intensely acid soil. Except for sea coast planting, I would not consider the Chainferns of as much value as the larger, handsomer species from the mountains.

Index of Scientific Names

The nomenclature used in this book is according to "standardized plant names" as they were in 1933. Changes in the scientific names are shown in the index after the word "now".

Aconitum uncinatum   49
Acorus calamus   95, 102
Actaea alba (now Actaea pachypoda)
   11, 68, 83, 126
Actaea rubra   11, 68, 83, 126
Adlumia fungosa   49
Anaphalis margaritacea   80, 81
Anemone canadensis   12, 43, 76, 105
Anemone cylindrica   12, 87
Anemone quinquefolia   12, 44
Anemonella thalictroides   44
Apios tuberosa (now Apios
americana)   13, 88
Aquilegia caerulea   52
Aquilegia canadensis   6, 15, 52
Aquilegia crysantha   53
Aralia hispida   84
Aralia nudicaulis   65, 84
Aralia racemosa   84
Arethusa bulbosa   28
Arisaema dracontium   66
Arisaema triphyllum   11, 15, 66, 126
Asarum canadense   15, 44
Asarum shuttleworthi   15
Asclepias incarnata   95, 102
Asclepias tuberosa   12, 57
Aster cordifolium   14, 119
Aster ericoides   14, 119
Aster linnaeafolia   14, 120
Aster novae-angliae   14, 76, 120
Aster novibelgi   14, 119
Aster puniceus   14, 89, 119
Aster spectabilis   14, 120
Aster umbellatus   14, 120

Baptisia australis   59
Baptisia bracteata (now Baptisia
leucophaea)   59
Baptisia leucantha   59

Baptisia tinctoria   59

Calla palustris   89
Callirhoe involucrata   59
Callirhoe triangulata   59
Caltha palustris   15, 89, 95, 102, 107
Calopogon pulchellus   27, 63, 101
Calypso bulbosa   15, 78
Camassia esculenta (now Camassia
scilloides)   80
Campanula pumila   123
Campanula rotundifolia   11, 53
Cassia marilandica   95, 102
Caulophyllum thalictroides   66
Chelidonium majus   84
Chelone glabra   91, 99
Chelone lyoni   91
Chimaphila maculata   107
Chimaphila umbellata   107
Chiogenes hispidula   7, 12, 15, 81, 107
Cicuta maculata   83, 95
Cimicifuga americana   44
Cimicifuga racemosa   44
Claytonia virginica   13, 15, 53
Clintonia borealis   66, 105
Clintonia umbellulata   7, 13, 67
Clintonia uniflora   67
Coptis trifolia (now Coptis groenlandica)
   7, 93, 105
Coreopsis lanceolata   76
Cornus canadensis   7, 66, 67, 85, 105
Corydalis glauca   53
Corypantha vivipara (now Corypantha
mamillaria)   123
Cypripedium acaule   7, 13, 17, 19, 73
Cypripedium acaule alba   13, 19
Cypripedium arietinum   13, 15, 19
Cypripedium californicum
   13, 15, 17, 20

Cypripedium candidum   13, 15, 16, 17, 20, 101
Cypripedium montanum   13, 15, 20
Cypripedium parviflorum (now Cypripedium calceolus var. parviflorum)   20
Cypripedium pubescens   7, 13, 15, 20, 89
Cypripedium spectabile (now Cypripedium reginae)   7, 13, 15, 21, 89

Dalibarda repens   108
Decodon verticillatus   91
Delphinium tricorne   80
Dentaria diphylla   45
Dentaria laciniata   45
Dicentra canadensis   15, 52
Dicentra cucullaria   13, 15, 52
Dicentra eximia   11, 49
Dionaea muscipula   111, 113
Dodecatheon meadia   7, 12, 15, 81, 107
Drosera rotundifolia   111, 114

Echinacea angustifolia   80
Echinacea purpurea   80
Echium vulgare   75
Epigaea repens   7, 11, 12, 15, 31, 33, 73, 85, 105
Epilobium angustifolium   15, 59, 60
Epilobium angustifolium alba   60
Erigeron philadelphicum   76, 120
Erigeron pulchellus   120
Erythronium albidum   13, 15, 53
Erythronlum amerlcanum   13, 54
Erythronium californicum   13, 54
Erythronium citrinum   13, 54
Erythronium hendersoni   13, 54
Eupatorium coelistinum   45
Eupatorium perfoliatum   89, 95, 96, 101
Eupatorium urticaefolium (now Eupatorium rugosum)   45
Eupatorium purpureum   85, 89, 95, 96, 101, 102
Euphorbia corollata   12, 78

Filipendula rubra   76, 95

Galax aphylla   7, 108
Gaultheria procumbens   109
Gentiana andrewsi   8, 11, 84
Gentiana crinita   7, 8, 11, 101, 115, 117, 132
Gentiana linearis   8, 85
Geranium maculatum   54
Geranium robertianum   54
Gerardia virginica   45
Geum rivale   92
Geum strictum (now Geum aleppicum var. strictum)   92
Goodyera pubescens   15, 30
Goodyera repens var. ophioides   15, 30

Habenaria blephariglottis   14, 24, 89
Habenaria ciliaris   14, 23
Habenaria dilatata   24
Habenaria fimbriata   14, 24, 89, 95
Habenaria hookeri   24
Habenaria lacera   14, 23
Habenaria orbiculata   14, 25
Habenaria psycodes   14, 24, 89
Helianthus divaricatus   14, 87
Helianthus gigantea   14, 87
Hepatica acutiloba   7, 12, 13, 15, 55, 105, 126
Hepatica triloba   7, 12, 13, 15, 55, 105
Hibiscus moscheutos   95, 104
Hieracium aurantiacum   75
Houstonia caerulea (now Hedyotis caerulea)   61
Hydrastis canadensis   45
Hydrophyllus virginianum   45
Hypoxis hirsuta   63

Inula helenium   85
Iris cristata   15, 55, 105
Iris prismatica   95, 104
Iris pseudacorus   95, 104
Iris verna   7, 55
Iris versicolor   95, 104
Isopyrum biternatum   12, 46

Jeffersonia diphylla 6, 15, 46

Leucocrinum montanum 124
Lewisia rediviva 124
Liatris pycnostachya 14, 76
Liatris scariosa 14, 76
Liatris spicata 14, 76
Lilium canadense 6, 11, 14, 16, 73, 74, 76, 95
Lilium carolinianum (now Lilium michauxii) 11, 14, 74
Lilium grayi 11, 14, 16, 74
Lilium pardalinum 11, 74
Lilium parryi 11, 14, 74
Lilium philadelphicum 7, 11, 73
Lilium superbum 11, 14, 74, 95
Linnaea borealis americana 7, 12, 107
Liparis liliifolia 29, 89
Liparis loeselii 30, 89
Lithospermum canescens 76
Lobelia cardinalis 14, 95, 96
Lobelia syphilitica 97
Lupinus perennis 60
Lysimachia nummularia 12, 108
Lysimachia quadrifolia 91
Lysimachia terrestris 91
Lythrum salicaria roseum 102

Maianthemum canadense 46, 65, 105
Medeola virginica 65, 87
Mentha piperita 97
Mentha spicata 98
Mertensia virginica 13, 14, 15, 46
Mimulus ringens 95, 103
Mitchella repens 12, 13, 65, 105
Mitella diphylla 15, 54
Monarda didyma 85
Monarda fistulosa 87, 95
Monarda meadia 87
Moneses uniflora 47
Myosotis scorpioides 97, 98

Nelumbo lutea 15, 98
Nuphar advena 98
Nymphaea odorata 15, 98

Oenothera caespitosa 123

Oenothera speciosa 123
Opuntia fragilis 121
Opuntia polyacantha 123
Opuntia vulgaris (now Opuntia humisifusa) 121
Orchis spectabilis 7, 15, 29
Oxalis acetosella (now Oxalis montana) 48
Oxalis violacea 48

Panax quinquefolium 16, 68
Panax trifolium 93
Parnassia caroliniana (now Parnassia glauca) 103
Pedicularis canadensis 47
Penstemon barbatus 77
Penstemon digitalis 77
Penstemon grandiflorus 123
Penstemon hirsutus 77
Phlox amoena 13, 14, 70
Phlox bifida 13, 14, 71
Phlox divaricata 6, 12, 13, 14, 70
Phlox glaberrima 13, 14, 71
Phlox maculata 13, 14, 71
Phlox ovata 12, 13, 71
Phlox pilosa 13, 14, 70
Phlox reptans 7, 13, 14, 71, 105
Phlox subulata 13, 14, 70, 71
Physostegia speciosa (now Physostegia virginiana) 93, 95, 101
Phytolacca americana 15, 60, 65
Podophyllum peltatum 65, 109
Pogonia ophioglossoides 27, 101
Polemonium reptans 11, 48
Polygala paucifolia 12, 48
Polygonatum biflorum 67
Polygonatum commutatum (now Polygonatum canaliculatum) 67, 76, 95
Pontederia cordata 97
Potentilla tridentata 61
Pyrola americana (now Pyrola rotundifolia var. americana) 47
Pyrola elliptica 47

Ranunculus bulbosa 81
Ranunculus repens 104

Rhexia virginica   103
Rudbeckia hirta   60, 76
Rudbeckia newmanni   60

Sagittaria latifolia   97
Salvia azurea   61
Sanguinaria canadensis   10, 15, 52
Sanguisorba canadensis   95, 98
Sarracenia flava   7, 89, 111, 113
Sarracenia minor   7, 89, 111, 113
Sarracenia purpurea   7, 89, 101,
   111, 132
Sarracenia rubra   7, 89, 111, 113
Saxifraga pennsylvanicum   91, 101
Saxifraga virginiensis   56
Scutellaria integrifolia   103
Senecio aureus   92, 101
Shortia galacifolia   7, 108
Silene latifolia   75
Silene pennsylvanica (now Silene
   caroliniana var. pennsylvanica)   61
Silene stellata   78
Silene virginica   49
Sisyrinchium angustifolium   63
Smilacina racemosa   68
Smilacina stellata   68
Solanum dulcamara   65, 99
Solidago canadensis   78, 83
Solidago odora   78, 83
Spiranthes cernua   29, 101
Spiranthes plantagineum   101
Streptopus amplexifolium   16, 65
Streptopus roseus   65
Symplocarpus foetida   92

Thalictrum dioicum   84, 89
Thalictrum polyganum   84, 89, 95
Thermopsis caroliniana   14, 60
Tiarella cordifolia   7, 15, 54
Tradescantia bracteata   78
Tradescantia pilosa (now Tradescantia
   subaspera)   77
Tradescantia virginiana   77

Trientalis americana (now Trientalis
   borealis)   48
Trillium cernuum   11, 14, 41
Trillium erectum   11, 14, 40
Trillium flavum   11, 14, 41
Trillium grandiflorum   11, 14,
   40, 65
Trillium nivale   11, 14, 39, 92
Trillium recurvatum   11, 14, 41
Trillium rivale   40
Trillium sessile californicum
   11, 14, 40
Trillium stylosum   11, 14, 41
Trillium undulatum   7, 11, 14, 41
Trollius laxus   93
Tussilago farfara   97, 98
Typha angustifolium   96
Typha latifolia   96, 101

Uvularia perioliata   87
Uvularia sessilifolia   15, 87

Veratrum viride   92, 101
Verbena hastata   95, 103
Vernonia altissima   95, 103
Veronica officinalis   49
Veronica virginica   78
Vinca minor   108
Viola blanda   15, 37
Viola canadensis   15, 37
Viola cucullata   15, 36
Viola palmata   15, 36
Viola papilionacea   15, 36
Viola pedata   15, 35
Viola pedata bicolor   15, 36
Viola pubescens   15, 36
Viola rotundifolia   15, 36

Waldsteinia fragaraoides   13, 109

Yucca glauca   123

Zizia aurea   88

138

Index of Common Names

Allspice, Carolina   14, 60
Anemone, American Wood   12, 44
Anemone, Candle   12, 87
Anemone, False Rue   12, 46
Anemone, Meadow   12, 43, 76, 105
Anemone, Rue   12, 44
Aralia, Bristly   84
Arbutus, Trailing   7, 11, 12, 15, 31, 33, 73, 85, 105
Arethusa   28
Arrowhead, Common   97
Asters   83
Aster, Blue Wood   14, 119
Aster, Flat-Top   14, 120
Aster, Heath   14, 119
Aster, Narrowleaved   14, 120
Aster, New England   14, 76, 120
Aster, New York   14, 119
Aster, Seaside   14, 120
Aster, Showy   14, 120
Aster, Swamp   14, 74, 119
Avens, Purple   92
Avens, Yellow   92

Baneberry, Red   11, 68, 83, 126
Baneberry, White   11, 68, 83, 126
Barren-Strawberry   13, 109
Beebalm, Oswego   85
Bellwort   87
Bishopscap, Common   15, 54
Bitterroot   124
Black-Eyed-Susan   60, 76
Bleedingheart, Fringed   11, 49
Bloodroot   10, 15, 52
Blooming Sally   59
Bluebell, Dwarf   123
Bluebells-of-Scotland   11, 53
Bluebells, Virginia   13, 14, 15, 46
Blue-Eyed-Grass   63
Bluets   61
Boneset   89, 95, 96, 101
Bugbane, American   44
Bugbane, Cohosh   44
Bunchberry   7, 66, 67, 85, 105

Burnet, American   95, 98
Buttercup, Bulb   81
Buttercup, Creeping   104
Butterflyweed   11, 57

Cactus, Brittle   121
Calla, Wild   89
Calypso   15, 28
Campion, Bladder   75
Campion, Starry   78
Cardinalflower   14, 95, 96
Cattail, Common   96, 101
Cattail, Narrowleaved   96
Celandine   84
Checkerberry   7, 65
Cinquefoil, Wineleaf   61
Climbing Fumitory   49
Clintonia, Speckled   7, 13, 67
Cohosh, Blue   66
Cohosh Bugbane   44
Coltsfoot, Common   97, 98
Columbine, American   6, 15, 52
Columbine, Colorado   52
Columbine, Golden   53
Coneflower, Narrowleaf   80
Coneflower, Purple   80
Coreopsis, Lance   76
Corydalis, Pale   53
Cowlily   98
Crinkleroot   45
Cucumber-Root   65, 87
Culvers Root   78

Dalibarda, Creeping   108
Devil's Paintbrush   75
Dragon, Green   66
Dragonhead, Tall Cluster False   93, 95, 101
Dragonroot   66
Dutchmans-Breeches   13, 15, 52

Elecampane   85
Evening-Primrose   123
Evening-Primrose, Tufted   123

139

Everlasting, Pearl   80, 81
Eyebright   61

False-Dragonhead, Tall Cluster   93,
   95, 101
False-Hellebore, American   92, 101
Firepink   49
Firewood   15, 59, 60
Fleabane, Philadelphia   76, 120
Flytrap, Venus   111, 113
Foamflower   7, 15, 54
Forget-Me-Not, True   97, 98
Foxglove, Wild False   45
Fringe, Mountain   49
Fringe-Orchid, Large Purple   24
Fringe-Orchid, Large Roundleaved   25
Fringe-Orchid, Ragged   23
Fringe-Orchid, Small Purple   24
Fringe-Orchid, White   24
Fringe-Orchid, yellow   23

Galax   7, 108
Gayfeather, Button   14, 76
Gayfeather, Cattail   14, 76
Gayfeather, Spike   14, 76
Gentian, Closed   8, 11, 84
Gentian, Fringed   7, 8, 11, 101,
   115, 117, 132
Gentian, Narrowleaved   8, 85
Geranium, Wild   54
Ginseng, American   16, 68
Ginseng, Dwarf   93
Globeflower, American   93
Goldenrod, Canada   78, 83
Goldenrod, Fragrant   78, 83
Goldenseal   45
Goldeye-Grass   63
Goldthread   7, 93, 105
Greek-Valerian   11, 48
Groundnut   13, 88
Groundsel, Golden   92, 101

Harebell   53
Hawkweed, Orange   75
Hellebore, American False   92, 101
Hepatica, Roundlobe   7, 12, 13, 15,
   55, 105

Hepatica, Sharplobe   7, 12, 13, 15, 55,
   105, 126
Herb Robert   54
Hyacinth, Wild   80

Innocence   61
Ironweed, Tall   95, 103
Iris, Blueflag   95, 104
Iris, Crested 15, 55, 105
Iris, Cubeseed   95, 104
Iris, Vernal   7, 55
Iris, Yellowflag   95, 104

Jack-in-the-Pulpit   11, 15, 66, 126
Joe-Pye-Weed   85, 89, 95, 96, 101, 102

Ladies-Tresses, Nodding   29, 101
Ladies-Tresses, Wide-leaved   101
Ladyslipper, California   13, 15, 17, 20
Ladyslipper, Common Yellow   7, 13,
   15, 20, 89
Ladyslipper, Mountain   13, 15, 20
Ladyslipper, Ramshead   13, 15, 19
Ladyslipper, Snowy   7, 13, 15, 21, 89
Ladyslipper, White   13, 15, 16, 17,
   20, 101
Larkspur, Rock 80
Lily, American Turkscap   11, 14, 74, 95
Lily, Canada   6, 11, 14, 16, 73,
   74, 76, 95
Lily, Carolina   11, 14, 74
Lily, Gray's   11, 14, 16, 74
Lily, Lemon   11, 14, 62
Lily, Leopard   11, 74
Lily, Meadow   6, 11, 14, 16, 73, 74,
   76, 95
Lily, Orangecup   7, 11, 73
Lily, Wood   7, 11, 73
Lobelia, Large Blue   97
Loosestrife, Fringed   88
Loosestrife, Rose   102
Loosestrife, Swamp   91
Loosestrife, Whorled   91
Lotus, American   15, 98
Lupine, Blue   60
Lupine, Sun-Dial   60

140

Marshmarigold   15, 89, 95, 107
Mayapple, Common   65, 109
Mayflower, Canada   46, 65, 105
Meadowbeauty, Common   103
Meadowrue, Early   84, 89
Meadowrue, Tall   84, 89, 95
Meadowsweet, Prairie   76
Merrybells, Little   15, 87
Merrybells, Wood   87
Milkweed, Swamp   95, 102
Mistflower   45
Mitrewort   15, 54
Moccasin Flower, Pink   7, 13, 17,
   19, 73
Moccasin Flower, White   13, 19
Moneywort   12, 108
Monkeyflower, Allegheny   95, 103
Monkshood, Clambering   49
Mountain Fringe   49
Myrtle, Blue   12, 109

Nightshade, Bitter   65, 99

Oconee-Bells   7, 108
Orchid, Grass-Pink   27, 63, 101
Orchid, Hooker   24
Orchid, Large Purple Fringe   14, 24,
   89, 95
Orchid, Large Roundleaved Fringe
   14, 25
Orchid, Ragged Fringe   14, 23
Orchid, Small Purple Fringe   14, 24, 89
Orchid, White Bog   24
Orchid, White Fringe   14, 24, 89
Orchid, Yellow Fringe   14, 23
Orchid, Snowy   7, 13

Parnassia, Carolina   103
Parsnip, Wild   88
Partridgeberry   12, 13, 65, 105
Peatpink   61
Penstemon, Eastern   77
Penstemon, Foxglove   77
Penstemon, Shell-Leaf   123
Penstemon, Torrey   77
Peppermint   97
Pepperroot   45

Periwinkle, Common   108
Phlox, Amoena   13, 14, 70
Phlox, Blue   6, 12, 13, 14, 70
Phlox, Cleft   13, 14, 71
Phlox, Creeping   7, 13, 14, 71, 105
Phlox, Downy   13, 14, 70
Phlox, Lovely   13, 14
Phlox, Moss   13, 14, 70, 71
Phlox, Mountain   12, 13, 14, 71
Phlox, Smooth   13, 14, 71
Phlox, Sweet William   13, 14, 71
Pickerelweed   97
Pipsissewa, Common   107
Pipsissewa, Striped   107
Pitcherplant, Common   7, 89, 101,
   111, 132
Pitcherplant, Hooded   7, 89, 111, 113
Pitcherplant, Sweet   7, 89, 111, 113
Pitcherplant, Trumpet   7, 89, 111, 113
Plantain, Creeping Rattlesnake   15, 30
Plantain, Downy Rattlesnake   15, 30
Plantain, Poor-Robins   120
Pogonia, Rose   27, 101
Pokeberry, Common   15, 60, 65
Polygala, Fringed   12, 48
Poppy-Mallow, Low   59
Potatobean   13, 88
Primrose, Evening   123
Primrose, Tufted Evening   123
Puccoon   76
Pyrola, One-Flowered   47
Pyrola, Roundleaf   47

Quaker Ladies   15, 61
Queencup   67

Ragwort, Golden   92, 101
Rosemallow, Common   95, 104

Salvia, Azure   61
Sarsaparilla, Wild   65, 84
Saxifrage, Swamp   91, 101
Saxifrage, Virginia   56
Senna, Wild   95, 102
Shinleaf   47
Shootingstar, Common   7, 12, 15,
   81, 107

141

Skullcap   103
Skunkcabbage   92
Snakemouth   27, 101
Snowberry, Creeping   7, 12, 65, 107
Solomonseal, False   68
Solomonseal, Great   65, 76, 95
Solomonseal, Small   67
Solomonseal, Starry False   68
Spatterdock   98
Spearmint   98
Speedwell, Common   49
Spiderwort, Bracted   78
Spiderwort, Virginia   77
Spiderwort, Zigzag   77
Spikenard, American   84
Spiraea, Pink   76, 95
Springbeauty, Virginia   13, 15, 53
Spurge, Flowering   12, 78
Squirrelcorn   15, 52
Starflower, American   48
Stargrass, Yellow   63
Starlily   124
Strawberry, Barren   13, 109
Sundew, Roundleaf   111, 114
Sunflower, Wild   14, 87
Sunflower, Woodland   14, 87
Swampcandle   91
Sweetflag   95, 102

Thimbleweed   87
Thistle, Blue   75
Thoroughwort, Snow   45
Toothwort, Cut   45
Trillium, California   11, 14, 40
Trillium, Dwarf   11, 14, 39, 92
Trillium, Nodding   11, 14, 41
Trillium, Painted   7, 11, 14, 41
Trillium, Prairie   11, 14, 41
Trillium, Purple   11, 14, 40
Trillium, Rose   11, 14, 41
Trillium, Snow   11, 14, 40, 65
Trillium, Yellow   11, 14, 41
Troutlily, California   13, 54

Troutlily, Common   13, 54
Troutlily, Henderson   13, 54
Troutlily, Lemon   13, 54
Troutlily, White   13, 15, 53
Turtlehead, White   91, 101
Twayblade, Lily   29, 89
Twayblade, Loesel   30, 89
Twinflower, American   7, 12, 107
Twinleaf   6, 15, 46
Twistedstalk   16, 65
Twistedstalk, Rosy   65

Vervain, Blue   95, 103
Violet, Birdsfoot   15, 35
Violet, Birdsfoot, Two-color   15, 36
Violet, Blue Marsh   15, 36
Violet, Butterfly   15, 36
Violet, Canada   15, 37
Violet, Downy Yellow   15, 36
Violet, Palm   15, 36
Violet, Roundleaf   15, 36
Violet, Sweet White   15, 37
Viper's Bugloss   75

Wakerobin   11, 14, 40
Waterhemlock, Spotted   83, 95
Waterleaf   45
Waterlily, American   15, 98
Wildbergamot   87, 95
Wildbergamot, Purple   87
Wildginger, Canada   15, 44
Wildginger, mottled   15
Wild-Indigo, Blue   59
Wild-Indigo, Cream   59
Wild-Indigo, White   59
Wild-Indigo, Yellow   59
Windflower   15, 44
Wintergreen   109
Woodbetony, Early   47
Woodsorrel, Common   48
Woodsorrel, Violet   48

Yucca, Soapweed   123

Ferns - Index of Scientific Names

Adiantum pedatum   126, 130
Asplenium platyneuron   126
Asplenium trichomanes   126, 127
Athyrium filixfemina   127
Athyrium pycnocarpon   127
Athyrium thelypteroides   127

Botrychium obliquum   127
Botrychium virginianum   127

Camptosorus rhizophyllus   6, 125, 128
Cystopteris bulbifera   128
Cystopteris fragilis   128, 133

Dennstedtia punctilobula   126, 128, 129
Dryopteris clintoniana   129
Dryopteris cristata   101, 129
Dryopteris goldiana   89, 129
Dryopteris hexagonoptera   130
Dryopteris linnaeana   125, 126, 130
Dryopteris marginalis   126, 130
Dryopteris noveboracensis 101, 130
Dryopteris phegopteris   126, 129
Dryopteris spinulosa   130
Dryopteris thelypteris   101, 126, 130

Lygodium palmatum   126, 131

Onoclea sensibilis   89, 101, 131, 132
Ophioglossum vulgatum   131
Osmunda cinnamomea   95, 101, 125,
   132, 134
Osmunda claytoniana   95, 125, 132
Osmunda regalis   89, 95, 101, 125,
   132, 133

Polypodium vulgare   126, 133
Polystichum acrostichoides   125,
   130, 133
Polystichum braunii   125, 133
Pteretis nodulosa (now Matteuccia
   struthiopteris)   95, 125, 134
Pteridium aquilinum   133

Scolopendrium vulgare   128

Woodsia ilvensis   134
Woodsia obtusa   134
Woodwardia areolata   89, 126, 134
Woodwardia virginica   89, 126, 134

Ferns - Index of Common Names

Adderstongue, Common   131

Beechfern, Narrowleaf   126, 129
Bladderfern, berry   128
Bracken   133
Brittle Fern   128, 134

Chainfern, Narrowleaf   89, 126, 134
Chainfern, Virginia   89, 126, 134
Christmas Fern   125, 130, 133
Cinnamon Fern   95, 101, 125, 132, 134
Climbing Fern   126, 131

Goldie Fern   89, 129
Grapefern, Ternate   127

Hartford Fern   126, 131
Hartstongue   128
Hay-scented Fern   126, 128
Hollyfern, Braun   125, 133

Interrupted Fern   95, 125, 132

Lady Fern   127

Maidenhair, American   126, 130
Marshfern   101, 126, 130

New York fern   101, 130

Oakfern   125, 126, 130
Ostrich Fern   95, 125, 134

Polypody, Common   126, 133

Rattlesnake Fern   127
Royal Fern   89, 95, 101, 125, 132, 133

Sensitive Fern   89, 101, 131, 132
Spleenwort, Ebony   126
Spleenwort, Maidenhair   126, 127
Spleenwort, Narrowleaf   127
Spleenwort, Silvery   127

Walking Fern   6, 125, 128
Woodfern, Clinton   129
Woodfern, Crested   101, 129
Woodfern, Evergreen   126, 130
Woodfern, Leather   126, 130
Woodfern, Toothed   130
Woodfern, Winged   130
Woodsia, Common   134
Woodsia, Rusty   134

An Important Message from the Publisher

Certain species of wildflowers are protected under the law and should not be taken from the wild. These include ladyslippers and trilliums, especially the Pink Ladyslipper (*Cypripedium acaule*) and the Snow or White Trillium (*Trillium grandiflorum*). Although some nurseries sell plants of these species and call them "nursery-grown," they are often actually gathered from the wild and kept in nursery holding areas for no more than several weeks or months. Commercial propagation of these species is not feasible, and gardeners should avoid buying such specimens. Please see paragraphs 4 and 5 of the Foreword by Henry W. Art.

ADVERTISEMENT
